TELL IT
TO WOMEN

AFRICAN AMERICAN LIFE SERIES
A complete listing of the books in this series
can be found online at wsupress.wayne.edu

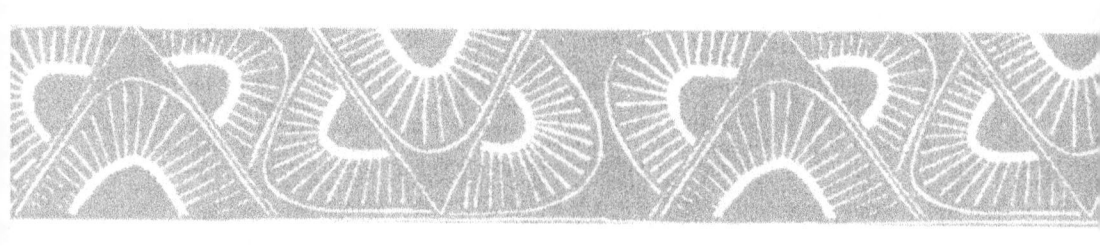

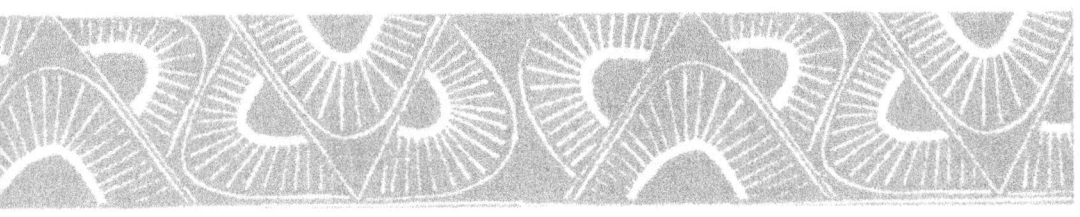

TELL IT TO WOMEN

AN EPIC DRAMA FOR WOMEN

Osonye Tess Onwueme

Foreword by Ngũgĩ wa Thiong'o

Wayne State University Press

Detroit

COPYRIGHT © 1994, 1997 BY OSONYE TESS ONWUEME. PUBLISHED BY WAYNE STATE UNIVERSITY PRESS, DETROIT, MICHIGAN 48201. ALL RIGHTS ARE RESERVED. NO PART OF THIS BOOK MAY BE REPRODUCED WITHOUT FORMAL PERMISSION.

ISBN-13: 978-0-8143-2649-7   ISBN-10: 0-8143-2649-8

LIBRARY OF CONGRESS CATALOGING-IN-PUBLICATION DATA

ONWUEME, OSONYE TESS.

TELL IT TO WOMEN : AN EPIC DRAMA FOR WOMEN / OSONYE TESS ONWUEME : FOREWORD BY NGŨGĨ WA THIONG'O.

P. CM. — (AFRICAN AMERICAN LIFE SERIES)

ISBN 0-8143-2649-8 (PBK. : ALK. PAPER)

1. WOMEN—AFRICA—DRAMA. I. TITLE. II. SERIES.

PS3565.N85T45 1997

822—DC21 —DC21

[822]   97-450

                                     CIP

INQUIRIES REGARDING PERMISSION TO REPRESENT, REPRODUCE, PRODUCE, OR ACT ANY PART OF THIS PLAY SHOULD BE DIRECTED TO OSONYE TESS ONWUEME, DISTINGUISHED PROFESSOR OF CULTURAL DIVERSITY AND PROFESSOR OF ENGLISH, UNIVERSITY OF WISCONSIN, EAU CLAIRE, WI 54701.

TO YOU—
FOUNTAIN,
KING-MAN-DADA!
OBIKA—
KING-MAN-DADA!
   ALWAYS,
      YOUR "T"...

FOREWORD

Ngũgĩ wa Thiong'o

Many dramatic narratives about women and men in Africa tend to look at each as a uniform gender. Women, on the whole, are seen as victims of tradition, which, because of its roots in patriarchy, is often evoked by men as a justification for whatever they demand from women. Thus, more often than not, it is women who are expected to conform to time-hallowed customs, even when these have been emptied of their content. Tradition is often associated with rural culture, and it is contrasted with modern culture, which in turn is linked to urban and Western cultures. In such schema, tradition and modernity are in eternal opposition, and progress is seen as a leap forward from tradition to modernity. There is nothing in between, no selective borrowing and rejection; tradition and modernity are two polarities, always at war. In *Tell It to Women*, Osonye Tess Onwueme goes beyond the surface of the two polarities to examine their manifest realities in postcolonial Africa.

She looks at postcolonial Africa from the viewpoint of the rural women, those who till the land, those who have "the power to make and unmake the land," as Yemoja, one of the central characters, puts it. In so doing, Onwueme is able to examine the many burdens the African woman has to bear, particularly the burdens associated with traditionalism and class domination. Traditionalism is not the same thing as tradition. Traditionalism is a way of appealing to rules and customs—even when they have been drained of their meaning and content by time and changed circumstances—simply because this is the way things have always been done. At the center of traditionalism and colonialism, even postcolonialism, is a system of patriarchy that privileges men. But where in precolonial society there were checks and balances ensuring that gender roles did not translate into the economic and political impoverishment of women, in the colonial and postcolonial eras the burdens of race, class and external influences and control compound those of gender. In the colonial and postcolonial eras middle-class women may very well share some aspects of gender oppression with peasant women. But as members of the dominant social stratum they share all its prejudices and attitudes, including negative attitudes toward rural culture, where the majority of women reside. For, by and large, this dominant social stratum is urban based and Western educated; it is the basis of the government and the bureaucracy of the new states.

Ruth, a feminist scholar, and Daisy, a government official, belong to that stratum. They espouse the noble aim of bringing about better life for rural women. This aim is applauded by the rural women, who initially accept the leadership of Ruth and Daisy. For they too want to improve their lot. They want to share in the benefits of modern science and technology. But it becomes obvious in the course of the action that Ruth's and Daisy's ideas about progress and development are very different from those of the rural women. For Ruth and Daisy, progress is directly related to their notion of a Western-based, global sisterhood and to their needs as middle-class African women. They clearly equate their middle-class problems with those of women as a whole. Their own narrow class needs become the needs of the entirety of women. By starting from the universality of global sisterhood—and, in fact, remaining there—their understanding of rural women becomes a matter of slogans and abstractions about gender rights and equality. Their middle-class prejudices make them despise the reality of rural women living in their midst. Rural culture represents the past which they want to put behind them. From their perspective, rural culture is little more than a reserve of cheap labor and endless source of maids, the most oppressed sector of the hewers of wood and carriers of water.

But what emerges from the drama is the capacity of rural women to organize themselves and express their own needs. They have a balanced attitude toward patriarchy and traditions. They know the weaknesses and the strengths. They do not want to break with their history as if it has nothing to offer. They want to add to it: they want to borrow the best from modern science and technology while discarding what is anti-women in their own traditions. They want creative changes, not wanton destruction. As Tolue puts it, what they are looking for in the notion of the better life is to add "the wisdom of the new people to our own . . . new things to our life . . . not taking away the good things we already have. . . ." They want cooperation between men and women and not perpetual warfare. But women must be equal partners in defining the common agenda and, more importantly, women have to define their place in it. They want to be actors in the economic, political and social drama shaping their lives. In this they have to rely first and foremost on their own organized strengths. Thus the

FOREWORD

journey of the women from the village to the capital for the launching of the "Better Life for Rural Women" program becomes not only an outward journey—during which the middle-class pretensions of the postcolonial middle class are exposed as merely neocolonial—but also an inward journey toward rediscovering their selves, their strengths and their capacities. They realize that they are the ones who produce what the cities consume. Their dance in the last movement includes the unveiling of various products from Idu: yams, cassava, beautiful hand-woven cloths and other things that women have made. Their experience in the city and their new self-knowledge are summed up by Yemoja as she addresses Sherifat, Daisy's mother-in-law: "You know it is a dangerous jungle out here. We have seen and felt it together. We have a home. We have a place. Let us return to Idu where we know the texture of the land." In realizing that they, the rural women, are indeed "the women," and that they are the sea and land, they reject the leadership of those with a different class agenda. They now see and accept the necessity and the wisdom of generating their own leadership with a continuity that stretches all the way from the 72-year-old Adaku to 10-year-old Bose. One of the most moving scenes in the dramatic narrative is Yemoja's and Sherifat's transformation of Bose into the new masquerade and the symbol of the new yam. She is the future, marrying the positive aspects of tradition with the positive aspects of urban experience.

There are many other questions raised in this drama, including the value of abstract theorizing versus concrete reality and the issue of lesbian relationships. *Tell It to Women* is the first dramatic text from Africa to break the literary silence on issues of homosexuality. What is negative about Ruth and Daisy is not so much their lesbian liaison but rather their ideological class position. They do not see anything creative in national initiatives from rural culture; their visions for the women do not go beyond imitations and parroting of Western theories. In rejecting the rural women, Ruth and Daisy reject the unity of the sea and earth which is the basis of all life. Thus their activities and visions are life-negative rather than life-positive, the very opposite of the activities and visions of the rural women.

In all her work, Onwueme has shown daring in her exploration of ideas, even when they lead to subjects and themes which may seem taboo. She has a way of using images to express very crucial ideas. For example, in *Legacies*—where Ikenga is split into two halves—she explores important pan-African themes and sums up the historical tragedy of the first major division of Africa into continental and diasporan entities. Wholeness will come when the two halves come together.

Tell It to Women raises to a new level the daring and the intellectual range of her work. But there is also an unmistakable continuity. One of the most important links to her earlier writing is her continued exploration of the empowerment of African women. Here, as in *The Reign of Wazobia*, she raises questions of organization and political power. Only through organization and the consequent seizure and control of a measure of political power can any social group begin to dictate the uses to which that power is put. Rights are not given. They are asserted and defended, and this is necessarily a question of power. In this sense, Onwueme is eminently a political dramatist, for power affects every other aspect of a society. She explores these themes with a dazzling array of images and proverbs. Her drama and theater are a feast of music, dance, mime, proverbs, and story-telling. With *Tell It to Women*, Onwueme consolidates her position among the leading dramatists from Africa.

TELL IT
TO WOMEN

SETTINGS

From Idu Kingdom to the city.

CAST OF CHARACTERS

- **Daisy:** 40 years old. A Western-educated woman, Director of Women's Affairs in Government.
- **Ruth:** 41 years old. A feminist scholar, closely attached to Daisy.
- **Okei:** 45 years old. Daisy's husband, Secretary to Government.
- **Yemoja:** 34 years old. Semi-literate rural woman and devotee of Onokwu/Yemoja, Goddess of the Sea. She is Koko's wife and has been elected by the Umuada, the daughters of the land of Idu, to represent the village at the launching in the city of the "Better Life for Rural Women" program.
- **Koko:** 42 years old. Semi-literate rural man, Yemoja's husband.
- **Ajie:** 74 years old. A farmer, Yemoja's father-in-law.
- **Ajaka:** 63 years old. A rural woman, Yemoja's mother-in-law.
- **Sherifat:** 61 years old. Daisy's rural mother-in-law and Okei's mother.
- **Tolue:** 60 years old. Yemoja's rural mother.
- **Adaku:** 72 years old. She is Omu (female king of Idu) and the Ada or oldest among the Umuada, daughters of the clan.
- **Bose:** 10 years old. Precocious daughter of Daisy and Okei.
- **Okeke:** 75 years old. Yemoja's rural uncle.
- **Her Excellency:** 40 years old. Wife of the president.

MOVEMENT ONE
Fatal Attraction—The Village Belle in Love with the Beautiful Monster

Stage is half-open; it is twilight, rather hazy, and nothing is distinct except for the voices of several women in the background, chanting or repeating after some other voices.

VOICES:
> The launching comes up soon. The word for now is BETTER LIFE FOR RURAL WOMEN!

OTHER VOICES: *(Repeating.)*
> Beta Laif for lulal women!

VOICES:
> Again?

OTHER VOICES: *(Repeating.)*
> Beta Laif for lulal women!

(The mood changes as the women break into a chant of "Yemoja! Yemoja! Yemoja!" We see female figures organizing themselves around a space that resembles the crossroads in a marketplace. At the center is the figure of a young woman who apparently is the subject of the chant, for the women have encircled her, drumming and chanting "Yemoja! Yemoja! Yemoja! Dance. Life is a dance. Dance, daughter, dance! Dance! Dance! Life is a dance!" They bounce her from one person to another, chanting "Dance, daughter, dance! Life is a dance! Dance, daughter, dance! This is your chance!" YEMOJA is bashful but soon warms up. The entire scene is filled with figures of women drumming, dancing and chanting.)

YEMOJA:
> I know life is a dance
> I know I must dance
> I know I must move with the dance
> I know I'm the new masquerade
> I know it is my chance
> Let me do my dance
> Let me move with the dance
> I know life is a dance

TELL IT TO WOMEN

I know it is a chance
Let me do my dance
Let me take my chance.

(*She arrives at center stage and begins to dance frenetically, with all the women, old and young, chanting "Yemoja! Yemoja!" as they disperse into the oncoming night. Suddenly, light floods the stage, which is forced open.*)

(*Light reveals YEMOJA alone as she wakes in a corner of DAISY's parlor. She starts and gropes with her hands, as if in search of her bearings. It is clear that she is disturbed, confused, and she darts her head from side to side to capture the voices around her. She rises slowly from the sleeping mat on the floor. Her mind is heavy as she searches for the women in her sleep, wondering where the women have gone. The firm tap of high-heeled shoes can be heard crossing the marble floor toward her little space by the corner of the living room, where DAISY has assigned her to sleep since her arrival in the city. Her only possession here is a raffia mat which she spreads on the floor of this room lavishly decorated with all kinds of artifacts imported from overseas. YEMOJA jumps up and begins dusting the chairs when DAISY enters. DAISY's eyes, hooded by artificially elongated lashes, emit such sparks of anger that YEMOJA trembles. DAISY's presence is so overwhelming that it is only after her initial blaze of words has burnt YEMOJA's fledgling pride and self-esteem that she notices RUTH standing behind DAISY and nodding to the "dressing-down" that DAISY is giving her. This dressing-down has become a ritual, for these elite women must ensure that the village woman understands her place in the scheme of things. Silence as DAISY and RUTH confront YEMOJA.*)

DAISY: (*Facing YEMOJA threateningly.*)
Yes, Her Excellency from Idu village! Still sleeping? Ahn? Sleeping! (*YEMOJA is silent.*) Well, go on and sleep and never stop! Woe to you if you do! (*YEMOJA turns.*) Look at the clock . . . that is, if you have any eyes. Tell me, what time is it? (*Silence.*) What does the time say? (*YEMOJA is still silent but shifts backward to avoid DAISY's menacing advancement.*) I'm talking to you! Tell me what the time says! (*YEMOJA is not only silent now, but increasingly nervous.*) You cannot tell what time says just as you cannot read the clock! You are not only dumb, you are blind as well! (*DAISY advances to slap YEMOJA, but RUTH's hand is already in place to arrest her.*)

RUTH:
No, Daisy, don't! These villagers are evil. Don't let them push you to the limit. You gotta be careful when driving on a road with animals crossing. . . .

DAISY:
I hear you, darling. I'm sorry. . . . (*Pause.*) Just that these idiots who

also call themselves women drive you crazy. But we gonna deal with them! (DAISY *turns to* YEMOJA.) Hey, QUEEN OF IDU! You know where you are? (*Silence.*) This is THE CITY! CITY! Not the cave you call home in the village! Understand? (YEMOJA *nervously nods in agreement.*) You do not know where you are, but I'm gonna tell you! That I offered to bring you to the city is no license for any reckless use of freedom. Understand? (YEMOJA *nervously nods in agreement.*) I've been watching you since you arrived here and I just can't wait anymore. . . . I can't wait to tell it. (*Pause.*) If you people think we make it by lying around here, you got to be kidding! City ain't like that. City's got its own rhythm. Understand? And you got a tail. There ain't no room for no monkey business here. The city ain't need no tail from rats like you 'cos your kind of tail too ugly and short to fit into the long body of this city. So get your dead butt off the ground or, better still, cut it off! No one is keeping any harems here. You don't run a corporation on some big butts but on some big bucks! Hard buck and bread! Understand? And that means the code here is hard work! Hard Work! Take it or leave it! Wait in that same spot and the limousines will soon be right on your doorstep to bring you the Better Life! Ugh! Better Life for Rural Women! We'll wait and see! You louse!!! (DAISY *throws her key at* YEMOJA. YEMOJA *ducks to avoid losing her eyes.* YEMOJA *is now panting. She tries to open her mouth to say something, stutters, then says nothing. Before she can make any further attempt,* DAISY *shuts her up with the thunder in her voice.*) I don't want to hear a word . . . not even one word from you. You think we're in contest or dialogue? Hey, her ladyship! There is no room for dialogue between us! (*Silence.*) Turn around and come over here! (YEMOJA *does not move.*) Come over here!

YEMOJA: (*Trying hard to hold back her tears.*)
Hmm . . .

RUTH: (*Breaking in.*)
Hmn . . . what do you mean! Is she your rank? Don't you know this woman standing before you here has a Ph.D.? And you better answer her 'YES, MADAM'!

YEMOJA: (*Cynically.*)
Yes, Medem! . . . Sorry, Medem! (YEMOJA *staggers and sulks out of the scene.*)

DAISY: (*Taking out her handkerchief.*)
You see now? See the thing you're trying to save? You should have let me give her that dirty slap so she'll wake up from her deep slumber. See her insolence? It's all happening right in front of you. I've been telling you this since we brought her here. These people are

just so crude, so senseless, and so irresponsible that the best thing to do is just not to bother with them. It's best to leave them as they are in their darkness. You'll break your arm trying to show them the light. And I ain't got no patience to smell their shit. You gotta know it: rural maids are nothing but stubborn pigs full of shit! . . . Excuse my language but that is what they are, these rural maids. . . .

RUTH: *(Correcting.)*
Rural women. . . .

DAISY:
Maids or women! Whatever they are . . . makes no difference. They are pigs . . . stubborn pigs. That is what they are. All their wealth is poverty . . . PO-VER-TY . . . breeding children whose legs can be measured against those of mosquitoes. And they're so backward that even if the hand of that clock was turned back a century, they wouldn't know the difference. Why? Because they're so fixed in their ignorance. I don't know why scholars like you spend all your energy theorizing and preoccupying your lives with trying to better the lives of these deadwoods. What on earth would improve the lives of these people who are so fixed in the past? Don't you realize that for them the present died in the past?

RUTH: *(Chuckling.)*
And not to talk of the future. . . .

DAISY:
I am really serious! These people are doomed! Can you imagine that this thing here is the best of them?

RUTH:
Well . . . maybe she needs time to adjust. . . .

DAISY:
I ain't giving no monkey no time to adjust its tail. I ain't giving no one time to adjust to idiocy! *(DAISY calls YEMOJA. YEMOJA enters and awkwardly tries to steady herself.)* Now hear this. You may be their "Queen" in that village. You might be the most high in the blind eyes of the Umuada, daughters of the clan. But know this here and now. You are NOTHING! Nothing . . . not even good enough to be a messenger in my office. We do have some serious code of conduct and order and how things should be done here. And we don't depend on "nothings" to achieve our goals. You better get your eyes open. And if you doubt who the boss is here, just stay there slouching! It won't be too long before you know who the real boss is. *(RUTH pulls DAISY aside to whisper something into her ear.)*

RUTH: *(At the door.)*
Easy, babe. It's no use trying so hard to humanize these deadwoods.

Easy. I must take care of some important business. See you soon. (*Daisy opens the door for Ruth to exit.*)

YEMOJA: (*Aside.*)
Ogwugwu, God of Iron, will smelt your lips for your injustices to me!

DAISY: (*Returning.*)
Ehn? What did you say?

YEMOJA:
No-thing . . . nothing . . .

DAISY:
Then better hold your stinking breath!

YEMOJA: (*Stammering.*)
B . . . but . . .

DAISY: (*Interrupting immediately.*)
Hold it! I'm not asking your opinion on this or any matter! And make no mistake about it! You came here for orientation, education, and remember no one forced you into this. The point was clear from the beginning. You agreed to serve . . . to work for a living. So prepare to take up the mantle of leadership. Prepare to herd your crowd in the village. . . .

YEMOJA: (*Exploding.*)
But! But . . .

DAISY: (*Cutting in.*)
And I haven't finished with you . . . yet! (*Tense silence. Daisy quickly steps into the next room to bring out a list of rules and regulations, which she soon begins to read out to Yemoja. While she's out of sight, Yemoja curses and fumes.*)

YEMOJA:
Onokwu, my totem River Goddess, will pour dirty water in your belly! You think you have found a cow. You will see! I'm going to show you pepper. . . .

DAISY: (*Returning.*)
Were you talking to me?

YEMOJA:
No! No! How can . . . ? Not at all!

DAISY:
You dare not! (*Silence as Daisy studies Yemoja's countenance and the sudden change that is taking place.*) Hmm . . . better watch yourself here. (*Pause.*) From now on, you must know your place in this household. We are not . . . cannot be equal in any way in this house!

No way! Got it? *(Silence.)* So know your limits. Your rights freeze once you come near my refrigerator. Your duty is to cook, not steal the meals. And "I" will dish out the food for you and everyone else in this household. Note that you eat after me and my family. *(YEMOJA is silent, but protest is fast shaping up on her lips.)* Under no circumstance must you dig anything, spoon or fork or finger, into my pot of soup. Understand?

YEMOJA: *(Sarcastically.)*
Yes Ma'am . . . *(It is becoming more and more obvious that YEMOJA's protest is gathering force as her confidence returns to her.)*

DAISY:
By three o'clock in the morning, you are up. You start each day by ironing my daughter's clothes, mine and my husband's! Clear?

YEMOJA:
Yes Ma' . . .

DAISY:
Clean the house. Prepare the breakfast. Set the table for me and my family. Under no circumstance must breakfast be late in my house.

YEMOJA:
Yes Ma' . . .

DAISY:
Wash your hands clean! Always . . . always. . . . Do you hear the emphasis? CLEAN ALWAYS!

YEMOJA: *(Studying her hands.)*
Yes . . . but . . .

DAISY: *(Cutting her off.)*
And don't you go touching my food with those fingers of yours with which you go digging into your nose. . . .

YEMOJA:
Ma' . . . but . . .

DAISY:
And make no mistake straying into my bedroom, or that of my husband, for that matter! I do not share anything with you, least of all a husband! So, don't ever . . . ever encroach on my space!

YEMOJA: *(Exploding.)*
Now, how am I to clean it up if I can't get into . . .

DAISY:
Just stop there! Only with my permission!

YEMOJA:
Hmmm . . . *(Footsteps are heard. RUTH is at the door.)*

RUTH:

And under her supervision too! (*RUTH walks straight to the refrigerator in the kitchen, pulls out a bottle of wine, pours out some for herself and some for DAISY. Then she returns to the parlor. They start drinking.*) Note her words! (*Between sips of wine.*) You people from the village must learn a lesson or two about privacy and respect for human and individual rights!

DAISY:

This is not a communal house. . . .

RUTH:

It's the product of some hard-earned Dollar and Naira. You hear that?

YEMOJA:

Hmmm . . .

DAISY:

Control your steps. This is neither your village slum nor your mother's. . . .

YEMOJA:

My . . . my . . . mother . . .? (*Before YEMOJA can pronounce the next word, DAISY has turned her back, pulling RUTH's hand after her as they walk with all their majestic arrogance upstairs, slamming the door after them. YEMOJA is now alone, battling between flashes of this deadly reality and the glamour of the beginning. Hot tears begin to roll down her face. She begins to dust the chairs.*) OH! So this is it! The city and all the shining lights . . . I . . . we saw from a distance? Whoever told me that it was going to come to this? (*Pause.*) And these women? These women? Tossing me about like a piece of rag? (*She returns to her sleeping mat and seats herself slowly on it. Pauses as she studies the scene around her. She searches and soon fixes her eyes on the plaque that was presented to her in the village by these same urban women. YEMOJA picks up the plaque, her hands trembling as she studies it. She turns it around and around as she reads the inscription aloud.*) "First steps to woman's freedom." (*She sighs. And then she explodes, tears freely flooding her face.*) So this is it! This is it . . . my bondage in freedom? (*Pause.*) With this, they bonded me? How would I know? How am I to know that women are not the same? How am I to tell the difference? (*Silence as she stares at the plaque.*) How would I know that when I accepted this, I was also accepting a new kind of chain? How is one to tell that there is so much beneath these gold-plated words and their worm-filled souls? They will answer to my totem Goddess, Onokwu. They will . . . the women will tell it to the River Goddess! (*Silence again as YEMOJA's eyes survey this new world.*)

So here I am! This is the bait! For this I turned away from my mother and father! For this I turned my back on husband and children? For this I sold all so that my name too will be written in gold, like this? Where am I to go now? If I return to my father, he will have no place for me. I'm already cursed. And I turned my back on all else to be here. And now this is what my life has turned into: another slavery. Slavery . . . slavery . . . another slavery. If I am not trapped in a husband's chain or father's chain, I'm trapped in another woman's chain. Where is the way? Where is the way? Where is the fre . . . free . . . freedom that these women talk about? Where is the freeeeeedom . . . ?

(Light snaps. Blackout.)

MOVEMENT TWO
A Dream Retold

YEMOJA *sobs until she falls into a deep sleep and begins to dream. In her dream, she is back in Idu. It's the first ritual in preparation for the celebration of the new yam festival in Idu at the beginning of the moon cycle. Festive atmosphere, gathering of women. For the most part, traditional dances of maidens, wives, and daughters of the clan all converge. There is definitely an air of excitement as drum sounds blend with the heavy feet of women of all ages dancing and denting the earth with the new energy of a new dance step. The dances go on for a while, but from time to time, one can hear discordant notes of protest from men gathering in the near distance. It is the droning voice of the men of Idu, denouncing this unusual gathering that is empowering the women and threatening the age-old stability of "the traditional family set-up," as the men would say. The backdrop screen reflects this scene of protest, which is in sharp contrast to the apparently harmonious spirit of women gathered for this all-important occasion when urban and rural women meet. Soon the music quiets down. The women begin to take their seats according to their age and status in the community. One young woman in the crowd looks different: you cannot tell whether she is urban or rural. She is* YEMOJA, *currently a fervent devotee of Onokwu, Goddess of the Sea and of Child Wealth. Onokwu is also called Yemoja.* YEMOJA, *the young woman, was once a student at a teacher training college but has fallen by the wayside as tuition fees increased and her parents had to choose which child to keep in school,* YEMOJA *or her younger brother. The choice was obviously her brother, since he was a male and* YEMOJA *was already old enough for marriage.* YEMOJA *has been resigned to her fate until now, but she has been hopeful that her own children would never have to face similar circumstances.* YEMOJA *married a court clerk, who had little to do in the village except read and write letters for people. This day, however, offers so much for* YEMOJA. *Today* RUTH *and* DAISY, *two modern, educated women, will arrive to speak to the assembled crowd; their appearance has a very special meaning for* YEMOJA. *The presence of these ultra-modern women will soon set off a replay of memories and emotions, as she recalls what she hoped to be and never became.* YEMOJA *sees* RUTH *and* DAISY *as images of herself outside her own immediate world. As the lights reveal,* YEMOJA *has a sour look about her that distinguishes her from the other village women who never had any formal education. Light moves away from* YEMOJA *to rest on two very talkative elderly women,* SHERIFAT *and* ADAKU. ADAKU *in particular has a truly ancient look about her.* SHERIFAT *chews away at her Kolanut, after throwing a few pieces onto Ani, the Earth Goddess, chanting incantations and imploring the goddess to sustain, nurture and open up their vision in Idu.* SHERIFAT *then shares the remaining pieces of Kolanut with* ADAKU *next to her.* ADAKU *takes a bite of her own piece of Kolanut and tucks the remaining piece into the upper corner of her right ear. She has Uli tattoos on her face and her arms, giving away her age as somewhere in her early seventies. But she still looks fairly strong and well coordinated for her age.* SHERIFAT *wears some kind of blouse, but the straps of her oversized handmade brassiere are so high up that the brassiere is way above her blouse and is the most prominent feature about her, besides her chattering away with old* ADAKU. *The other women who can be identified in the crowd are* YEMOJA's *mother,* TOLUE, *and other rural women who have never traveled out of Idu. There is a look of excitement on their faces as they sit, drums still throbbing in the background.* ADAKU *and* SHERIFAT *are obviously the center of focus for some time.*

ADAKU: (*To* SHERIFAT.)
> I knew it would happen some day. But I didn't know it would happen in my life.

SHERIFAT:
> Hmm, our mother. The gods are kind to us. I know they will smile on us. How can our gods and ancestors close their ears to our pleas for better days?

ADAKU:
> Before our very eyes, they have taken our own sons to go and fight out there in eh . . . eh . . . what do they call it now?

YEMOJA: (*Within earshot, supplies the answer.*)
> India and Burma, Mother.

ADAKU AND SHERIFAT: (*Excitedly.*)
> Ehn! My daughter.

ADAKU:
> You see? Our daughters raised from this very soil supplying answers to our questions? God be praised!!

SHERIFAT:
> That is why my heart foams like new palm wine on a hot afternoon, because of what we are experiencing this very day.

ADAKU:
> I knew it would happen! Our daughters will one day speak for us. Our people say that "your mouthpiece is your child." That is why we have children: that our children will be greater than we are. That is always our prayer . . .

SHERIFAT: *(Interrupting.)*

But the female child is more valuable. That I can defend anytime. Look at me now in my old age. It's my daughters who know that I need fish, crayfish, firewood, and soap for me to wash my clothes now. My rattling bones compete with the pestle....

ADAKU:

Are you telling me? "Nwanyi-bu-ife." The female child is truly something of treasure. Look at me now! Five male children! They throw plenty of money at me, as if money will answer my call. When I was younger I was filled with pride that I had so many sons. And of course, I had a special place in my husband's heart because I gave him the yam seeds for his lineage. You all here commonly call me "Obi Diee"—the one who knows the heart of her husband. Where is all that now? He gave me a special place among his other wives who had so many daughters. That is why you people with daughters don't know what your god has done for you. "Aku-aza-oku": wealth cannot answer the rich man's call no matter how much of it he has. That is why we value children more than anything else in our own world here. But our world is no longer what it used to be. Enu ofuu—New world ... Oyibo rules our world: they have ruined our world. Modern ways come with this thing—money, money, money.

SHERIFAT:

And our people are now running after it like ...

ADAKU:

Hmm! Is it that one you are saying? Our sons who go out there no longer remember us. They come back from far away speaking in tongues we cannot understand. Some of them even come back with white women as wives. You remember Dede's son who came back with this white woman ... eh ... what do they call that place now ... eh ... eh ...

SHERIFAT: *(Helping.)*

"Fa-lan-si!"

ADAKU:

Ehn! Falansi! The woman was so skinny; just bones. And when she visited us here in the village, you couldn't tell whether it was some stick cracking or her feet like those of a kite. I tell you, in spite of her youth (at least so our son said) her bones rattled so much, even my own sounded like child's play. And you would have thought those were sounds from rattle beads! *(The women laugh.)*

SHERIFAT: *(Helping.)*

And the worst thing is that she was speaking so much from her nose like some ghost from beyond. We all kept wondering what could have broken her nose inside! Even when some of our people who have mastered the white man's language spoke to her, she kept saying . . . ehm . . . ehm . . . (ADAKU *nudges* YEMOJA *on the shoulder.*)

ADAKU:
My daughter, what was it that white-bone Dede's son brought home used to say?

YEMOJA:
"Que-ce-que-se?"

ADAKU: (*Repeating.*)
Ehn! "Kasi-kasi." (*More laughter from the women.*) They say she spoke "Felenchi." Imagine a woman our son imports from the white man's country when our home is full of Assia . . . the best of the best fish? The woman was just illiterate like me. She didn't know "Twi" and she couldn't speak Ingrisi, just like me. Can't even write her name! Hmm, my children? Next moon, it will really shine!

SHERIFAT:
My sisters, power starts with the pen. Is it not because our daughters can write their names that they now ride in long cars?

TOLUE:
When Oyibo tells them come here they all go there. Wonders shall never cease! I never heard of Oyibo who could not speak English until Dede's son brought that bone home.

ADAKU:
So how come that Oyibo woman could not speak "Ingrisi"? Where was she when her men were learning? And come to think of it, I have never seen a white man that could not speak Oyibo.

SHERIFAT:
That woman is not the only one. I have heard of so many others. Where were the white women when their men were answering the school bell? (*Demonstrating.*) And she was such a sight with that wrapper tied around her waist as she hopped about like a frog! (*They all laugh.*)

ADAKU:
And what made me laugh more was that she really wanted to impress us by dressing like us.

SHERIFAT:
There is nobody I blame but our sons who have betrayed us to the white man. . . .

ADAKU: (*Pointing in the opposite direction.*)
Ahn! The moment has come. Our daughters are here! (*Everyone turns in this new direction. Two ultra-modern women walk majestically*

toward the crowd. They move with great confidence. They wear enough lipstick to paint a room. Their clothes look very expensive. There is no doubt at all that these women exude comfort, authority, power and control. The two male guards leading them to the gathering bow and hand over some files to each of them. Even though the rest of the people do not hear what the women are saying, it is obvious the men are taking instructions as they salute the women in military fashion. The crowd has been watching the entrance of these women with extreme admiration, and the moment these women receive the salute from the men, the crowd is ignited and rises as one, clapping and ululating with drum accompaniment. This euphoria empowers ADAKU's feet, and she lifts one after the other and then moves to a point that could be called the center of the circle. All the women turn their seats around so that everyone has a good view of her and is part of the circle. There are two special executive seats on the platform, and one of the younger women runs across to bring them forward for the special visitors. Everyone is now seated. ADAKU takes up her position at the center as the "Ada" of the clan. The Ada is a very important position of power, authority and respect among men and women. As the oldest daughter of the clan, she is "first among equals," the Umuada or the daughters of the clan. The Umuada are very powerful; they wield so much influence in the community that sons and other men of Idu can never rival or disrespect them. Umuada are, in fact, in command and control of the world, as well as the arrangements for this day. The other group of women who sit together, distinct from Umuada, are wives of the clan. You can tell from their manner that the women who are daughters of the clan exhibit much more confidence, authority and power than the women who are wives of the clan. A younger woman among the Umuada brings to the center a keg of palm wine and some Kolanuts. This is part of the ritual of the gathering of women, perhaps reflecting their role as earth mothers. ADAKU, taking up one of the Kolanuts from the bowl which the younger woman, YEMOJA, holds in front of her, calls on the gods and the ancestors. Then she takes up the kola as if offering it to the sky god.) Amadioha! God of the sky! Our God of justice! Idigwu! God of iron! Agwu!! Our God of creativity! Chukwu Abiemme, God almighty! God of creation! The one whose words never fail! Obida, Ngene's daughter, Sea Goddess whose breasts are so large they drop on her knees to feed the multitude of her children! Obida the supreme mother of justice, who can break the testicles of her erring sons! We salute you powers, seen and unseen!

CHORUS OF WOMEN:
   Iseeh, Onokwu, Yemoja, Goddess of the Sea!

ADAKU:
>The one whose waters yield abundant wealth! The one whose teeth are precious corals for the world's adornment! Onokwu, Yemoja, goddess whose womb is wide as the sea. Kindly yield us the children who will comfort our barren humanity.

CHORUS OF WOMEN:
>Iseeh!

>(*This rite completed, YEMOJA takes up the gourd for ADAKU to pour onto the earth and summon the ancestors and the gods and goddesses to bear witness to this gathering of their daughters from all directions. As in the initial rite, the women respond, "Iseeh may it be so" at each invocation.*)

ADAKU: (*Concluding the ritual.*)
>Ancestors! Our fathers and mothers! Those who have gone before us that our root may continue to be strong! Spirits! Gods and goddesses of Idu! Your daughters are here! The women are here! (*Calling on the crowd.*) Drums for women! (*Drum accolades follow, and the women exuberantly sing a very short, familiar tune as the drum rises to a high pitch. ADAKU, spiritually empowered, now shouts to the crowd.*) Chei-chei-chei Idu Kwenu!

CHORUS OF WOMEN:
>Eeih!

ADAKU:
>Kwenu!

CHORUS OF WOMEN:
>Eeih!

ADAKU:
>Kwenu!

CHORUS OF WOMEN:
>Eeieeeh! (*While the last response is drawn out, drum sounds are also prolonged, until every sound comes to an abrupt end, as if this were all prerehearsed. Brief silence. ADAKU now adjusts her wrapper and begins to address the gathering of women. From this moment onward, the echo of protests from the male gathering becomes more audible and frequent.*)

ADAKU: (*To the women of Idu.*)
>Daughters and women of Idu! The moment is here. The sun is high up. This is not a gathering of witches in the night or some secret society in broad daylight. This is our mid-season. The moon is half-grown. This is our season. The sun smiles on us. It's our time . . . especially those of us whose eyes have seen so many suns hide and blink their eyes . . . and then sleep forever. This is the moment we

have been waiting for since our heads were still the height of our knees. *(Her tone rises.)* Daughters of Idu, have we not waited long enough?

CHORUS OF WOMEN:
We have! *(This is followed by two drum accolades.)*

ADAKU: *(Continuing, but calmer now.)*
Now it's our time. After so many years of patching our clothes, patching our husband's clothes, patching children's clothes, washing, washing and washing by the river banks . . . our fingernails so short from frequent breaking . . . our heads going bald . . . from perpetual loads of water on our graying heads. Our feet getting smaller and smaller from eternal trudging to and from the stream to market, to farm, in search of life. At last, after so many seasons, "Gomenti"—the ones who rule us and turn our face so that we couldn't tell which hand was God's and which one was their human hands lashing at us. At last we shall reap the fruits. Look around you and see for yourselves. *(Pause.)* Something new and bright is here to bring light into our lives! *(All eyes turn to RUTH and DAISY, the ultra-modern guests from the city.)* At last our daughters have become our mouthpiece to "Gomenti." Is there not a saying among us in Idu that "If you begin to eat, you also give your sister and brother their share?"

CHORUS OF WOMEN:
That is true!

ADAKU:
Ehn! Our daughters are no different. They are true daughters of Idu. That is why they drum about our stomachs to the deaf ears of those who rule us.

CHORUS OF WOMEN:
Hmm . . . our sister . . .

ADAKU:
Our daughters know we are not primitive, not in this age. Women like us drive long, shiny cars, splashing mud and water on us as we beat the earth with our receding feet on our way from the market.

CHORUS OF WOMEN:
Hmm . . . our sister . . .

ADAKU:
Our daughters know that we too like to ride in long cars and fly like birds in the sky. Our daughters know that we long for clean water; that we too want to stand in the kitchen and turn metals to produce water to run into our bowls like the sky god pouring instant blessing into our bowl of life.

CHORUS OF WOMEN:
> That is true.

ADAKU:
> We long for light to shine all day long and all night long. We long for stars that close their eyes like those ones Osime saw when her daughter took her to the city.

CHORUS OF WOMEN:
> Eeih!

ADAKU:
> All this we have longed for in Idu for seasons. And now, our own daughters who know the languages of the powers on their fingertips, our own daughters stretch the arms of "Gomenti" to the extent that now they remember us! Because our daughters are here! The women are here, Idu! They say "Gomenti" has given them a package for us. *(Turning to* YEMOJA.*)* Say it for me, my daughter, since my teeth are falling and my tongue is too heavy to speak the white man's language!

YEMOJA: *(Rising.)*
> The program is "BETTER LIFE FOR RURAL WOMEN."

CHORUS OF WOMEN:
> What did you say!

SHERIFAT:
> Say it slowly, so we can hear!

YEMOJA:
> "Better Life for Rural Women." *(She is translating.)* "Nduoma"—new way to bring wealth to improve our lives.

CHORUS OF WOMEN:
> Ahn! May the gods hear them!

SHERIFAT:
> Now they are beginning to talk!!

ADAKU: *(Continuing.)*
> My daughters! I tell you, I do not hear "Ingrisi." But when I hear the word "aba-wu-tu" *(This is actually her reproduction of the word "about" as close as possible to Idu language.)* I know that thing has become too much. *(This brings general laughter into the crowd.)* Daughters and women of Idu! At last, those who rule us know we are abawuto. We are here. They can now see the wrinkles on our faces! This is our time! Our daughters are here! The women are here! Let them speak! *(Drum accolades follow* RUTH *and* DAISY *as they rise to the platform. The circle is now broken as all the women re-arrange themselves in rows to see and hear the modern women taking*

their place on the platform. RUTH opens her handbag, brings out a microphone and begins to speak. She speaks with a great deal of affectation, that brand of "oily English" in which every word and inflection is so drawn out that it sounds more "English" than the English. She wants to assure everyone in the audience that she is a "been-to" and that she has acquired a good dose of Western mannerisms. To leave the villagers in no doubt whatsoever, she repeatedly flicks her hair about; it is an exaggeratedly long, artificially implanted hairpiece with red and brown tints. Her partner, DAISY, is essentially the same, except that she speaks with a special American-flavored accent and carries off her affectation more convincingly than does RUTH. She imposes such nasalization on her speech that she seems to be speaking with her nose instead of her mouth. Having adjusted herself to the microphone, RUTH opens a folder, takes out her prepared speech and begins to address the audience.)

RUTH: *(Addressing the women of Idu.)*
 Idu!

CHORUS OF WOMEN:
 Eeih!

RUTH:
 I come to you as a pathfinder to show you the markers and centers from which women have been mystified, ostracized and marginalized for centuries.

CHORUS OF WOMEN: *(In admiration.)*
 Eeih!

VOICE FROM THE CROWD:
 Ugbana, our white bird! Beauty of beauties of birds in the forest! "FLY!" Fire! Our beautiful bird from the sky!

RUTH: *(Now more empowered by their approval.)*
 We are the torch bearers of global sisterhood. Our mission is to break boundaries of confinements and compartmentalization of our potentialities in the oppressive, despotic and tyrannical hegemony of patriarchy imposed on women these many years. . . .

CHORUS OF WOMEN:
 Eeih!

SHERIFAT:
 Go on! Fly, our daughter! Fly, our eagle Lutu!! *(Growing excitement among women.)*

ADAKU: *(Aside to SHERIFAT.)*
 What do you mean? Can you understand what she is saying?

SHERIFAT:
 Well, I cannot. But eh . . . can't you feel the way she rolls the words

on her tongue like yam in oil? Must one know Ingrisi to sense that she speaks it well?

ADAKU:

Sherifat, why do you see the oath and prefer instead to swear by the fire? Whatever she speaks, however well, it's not our tongue.

SHERIFAT:

What do I care that our daughters gain new voices?

ADAKU:

Why should you care? After all, one of them is your son's wife! Not mine!

SHERIFAT: *(Arrogantly.)*

And I am not ashamed of it either. Maybe you are jealous. And I know that you too once admired the way Oyibo was falling from her mouth like fire sparks from the bellows of a blacksmith.

ADAKU:

I see . . . we shall see how you handle that fire when we go to the city. They have come to invite us to the city. Isn't that it? We shall see then how the python basks in the sun!

SHERIFAT:

And I will bask with the python in the sun. If you are not tired of this village, I am. And I am ready to move with those who have the light that shines and bask with them in the sun. Tell me, who does a husband build a mansion for and she prefers instead to live in a shack? Let the truth shine. Our daughters have gained the power we did not have. Who says woman's power ends in the kitchen? See how she strides now, her body shining like looking glass, you can see with it. She certainly has learnt the white man's language well and can even teach it to him!

ADAKU:

There is no doubt about it.

SHERIFAT:

Boh, my sister. Who says education is not good? *(The noise continues. RUTH blows into the microphone to attract their attention. Her effort is in vain; rumblings, arguments among the women.)*

ADAKU: *(To SHERIFAT.)*

But too much Oyibo is not good either. It spoils the head. Don't you remember what all that Oyibo has done to crack the head of Eke's daughter? They say she reads too much; everything from newspaper, to book, to scraps of everything!! Until all that foreign knowledge scattered her brain and now she runs around naked in the streets of Benin. What use has the knowledge brought to her now?

RUTH: *(Struggling to continue her speech.)*
May I have your attention please? *(Her voice is drowned out by the noise.)*

SHERIFAT:
Adaku, that is Eke's daughter's business! The point is that she has not kept her hands clean. People who wander in foreign lands must also learn their norms and taboos and do the necessary rituals so they don't end up on the wrong path. It is the order of things. My sister at Abor who became converted to Christianity this year told me that their pastor has warned them that there are sections of that big book they call "Baibulu" that they must not read, or else it will make them mad.

ADAKU:
What if they read it?

SHERIFAT:
Oh! If you read it, you must first make some sacrifice. . . .

ADAKU:
You mean these educated Christians make sacrifices too?

SHERIFAT:
Oh yes! But theirs is scented. You know, not crude like ours here. The ritual of modern people is not our kind of ritual. Where we carry oil and fowl, these modern worshippers do not soil their hands. They first take plenty of money to the priest at the altar to say mass. And the holy communion they say is the body and blood of Jesus. The priest performs the ritual sacrifice on their behalf.

ADAKU:
What you are saying is that Christians also perform rituals like us. They may do it differently, pour perfume and incense not to have it smell, but it is all the same to me. Sacrifice is sacrifice whether you do it in the city or in the forest. Face the truth! Christians do ritual sacrifice!!

SHERIFAT:
What?

ADAKU:
I mean the sacrifice we do here and that one they do at the altar. . . .
(RUTH is now so impatient that she actually shouts into the microphone to get their attention. SHERIFAT, realizing that it is her duty to ensure order, swings her staff around.)

SHERIFAT: *(Shouting.)*
Order! The learned one wants to speak!! *(More rumbling from the women.)* Keep quiet! Let us hear the people who are people speak!

ADAKU:
> What do you mean "hear people who are people"? Are we not people? *(Somebody tries to stop her by pulling her down.)* Leave me. Let me speak my mind. Why should I fear? Is she not a woman like me? Does she carry more than one thing in her thighs? You people who see all these Oyibo and shake and wet your body with urine. . . . *(Aloud to RUTH.)* Yes, our sister from white man's land! We, the women of Idu, salute you. Your voice is so sweet and your tongue rolls the white man's language so smoothly like boiled yam in palm oil. But sister, your tongue sounds strange to us. Your words do not go down. Your words get stuck in our throat. And we do not understand you. *(AJAKA pulls at ADAKU's wrapper in an attempt to stop her.)*

AJAKA:
> That's enough now! Why are you opening our anus for the whole world to see? These people will soon begin to see us as illiterate.

ADAKU:
> As if they don't know we are illiterate. Now tell me, the one who steals another's drum, where is she going to beat it?

AJAKA:
> Hmm . . . I understand what you mean, but sometimes it is better not to open up for everyone to see where your Chi has branded you. It is better to let people discover for themselves and form their own impressions.

ADAKU:
> That is not the way, our way. There is a saying among us, "Eziokwu bunwa madu." Honesty is the mark of a good person of dignity. If you hide a disease, the disease hides you too. Haven't you heard of a white man who died in a gathering because his stomach was filled with gas and he was too ashamed to let it out? *(The women laugh.)* Ohoo! You see! If we must find a cure for our disease, these people must know our sickness.

AJAKA:
> Maybe you are right, our mother. They need to know where we are coming from.

SHERIFAT:
> But that does not mean we must break the eyeball because it itches. . . .

ADAKU: *(Charging at SHERIFAT.)*
> Enough! You dancer of fortune! Until today I thought I knew you to be strong. But now I know better; any wind blows you. And I am sure that even if this modern people had the skin of lizards you

would still lick their body . . . if only they would take you to the city. But I do not understand why our daughter must speak to us in the tongue of another.

CHORUS OF WOMEN: (*Applauding ADAKU.*)
Yes, our mother is right. (*They begin to protest to RUTH.*) Speak! Speak in a tongue that we know! (*DAISY and RUTH confer briefly. More noise among the women as they discuss the issue.*)

DAISY: (*Blowing through the microphone for attention.*)
Your attention, please! We have heard your complaint. But remember that our honorable guest left us so long ago. She is now like a stranger to this land. She cannot speak our tongue. We need an interpreter. . . . (*The women take up the chorus.*)

CHORUS OF WOMEN:
Yes, an interpreter! (*They look all around to see who among them best knows the strange language. Two people at once spot YEMOJA and point to her. All the women chorus her name, "Yemoja," as they lift her up to go forward and be the interpreter.*)

SHERIFAT: (*To YEMOJA.*)
Go Yemoja! Go Yemoja! Yemoja! (*YEMOJA rises shyly from her seat and steps forward to become their interpreter.*)

RUTH: (*Continuing.*)
As I was saying, our mission is the unification of women all over the world. . . .

YEMOJA: (*Clumsily, in their local language.*)
She says they have come together with all women: white women, yellow women, black women, big and small women, all to form one family.

CHORUS OF WOMEN: (*Excitedly.*)
Eeih!

RUTH:
The watchword for contemporary woman is EQUALITY. Time has come for redressing the female on the paradigmatic scale of being in equality with her male counterpart. (*YEMOJA mutters the words "contemporary" and "paradigmatic" jerkily and inaudibly, as she nervously tries to understand the concept herself.*)

YEMOJA:
She says, she says . . . that . . . that ehm . . . ehm . . . yes . . . she says there is no reason why men and women should not be dressed in the same way. That men and women are equal and . . . and . . . that . . .

CHORUS OF WOMEN:
We are listening. (*YEMOJA is obviously showing signs of uneasiness now.*)

RUTH:
> Indeed the time has now come for the redefinition and control of the dialectics of being. The feminist discourse is concerned with reinscribing and reconstructing the place of woman from the viewpoints of opposites. Women are to be centered against the background and parameters in logocentric and pedagogical terms, centers long appropriated by men, and all for the continued domination and suppression of women.... (*RUTH is waiting for YEMOJA to translate, but YEMOJA is so overwhelmed by the difficult syntax and vocabulary that she stutters increasingly, until finally all attempts at communication break down.*)

YEMOJA:
> Ehn... ehn... (*Turning to RUTH.*) Pardon? Please, say it again. (*RUTH repeats, but YEMOJA still struggles.*) She says that... that... women should... should now displace men and become rulers... and... (*Turning to RUTH.*) Honestly, these are the biggest English words I have ever heard in all my years. I can't... I just can't make sense out of this anymore.... (*Noise increases again. YEMOJA steps aside.*)

ADAKU: (*Aloud.*)
> I said it! Too much Oyibo is dangerous! Now the poor girl can't even hear her....

SHERIFAT:
> I'm surprised, for is this not the same Yemoja who writes and reads letters to us from our relatives living in the city?

ADAKU:
> Don't mind them. These shameless children who go abroad and lose their tongue. Tell me how they hope to come back and be any benefit to us?

SHERIFAT:
> But she spoke well. She spoke with power and she talks of power....

ADAKU:
> That too I have a problem with. What kind of power? Have we women of Idu not always had power? Look around you. Is this not a gathering of the Umuada and the wives of Idu?

SHERIFAT:
> You are right. But she is right too in her own way, and I can see her point... women's rights are limited....

ADAKU: (*Interrupting.*)
> As daughters? Don't we have rights as daughters?

SHERIFAT:
> Yes.

ADAKU:
As mothers? Don't we have rights as mothers?

SHERIFAT:
Yes. But what happens to us when we get married? Do we still have those rights? Tell me . . . what happens to our rights when we become wives?

ADAKU: (*Thinking.*)
Hmm . . .

SHERIFAT:
You see? That is the point!

ADAKU:
Maybe that is where they have a point.

SHERIFAT:
Our modern girls can see far. . . .

ADAKU:
Maybe that is where they have a point. But this thing about taking power from men and giving it to women is where I have a problem. Men have their own power and so do the women of Idu. If you now concentrate power in one part, male or female, think of the problem that will create in Idu. What becomes of the family? Will it not make worse the problem you are trying to solve?

SHERIFAT:
She says power will be distributed. With these Oyibo people, nothing is impossible. I have no doubt that if they say it, it will be done according to their will. And men and women will hold it equally. . . .

ADAKU:
Well, let me first say that anybody is free to dispose of their god and create or inherit any new god whenever they please. So I see you now worship these people . . . these Oyibo people. Maybe because of the material things they have to offer. Go on and worship your new gods. Adaku will not deviate from her own path; each one her own. But I still have a problem with you and these your new gods. How are they going to effect it in real life? How? So now women will have to sit back while the men conceive babies? (*SHERIFAT laughs.*) This is no laughing matter. For me, motherhood is the ultimate power, and I don't know any man yet born of woman who can boast of that power to conceive . . . I mean create and carry another life. In Idu, men are outsiders in the process of giving birth.

SHERIFAT:
How?

ADAKU: (*Vexed.*)
You surprise me, you know, Sherifat! Or is it that your son's wife,

who is one of them, has infected or converted you to their ways? You used to be more reasonable than this. I tell you, I too don't understand you anymore, even though you and I share the same family tree. How can an old woman like you be asking me that kind of question, like a little girl whose thighs have never been crossed by a man? Think of it: what happens in Idu when any woman is giving birth? *(Pause.)* All mothers gather around her to help her at the owelle, the private place for women's baths and where the child is born. What man dares encroach on that region at the child's birth or even afterward? Only women have such access and power to be part of the communal team to bring the child to life on behalf of the community. Even when the husband is around, he stays out and is only told after the baby is born. And that is because women believe that men are weak as far as this delicate process is concerned and therefore they must leave them out. While men exhibit their chivalry in the battlefield, women exhibit their own chivalry in the home. I know my world, and there is nothing any outsider can come and tell me to devalue it. How are they going to take away my sight and make me see my entire life with their own eyes?

SHERIFAT:
Well, that is what they are here to tell us. . . .

ADAKU:
Hmn! These new gods and goddesses. I do not trust them. I've been here too long to get carried away with these new promises without any real changes in our lives. What we want now is power . . . the power of money. That is the new power we seek to add to what we have!!

SHERIFAT:
But how are you going to have money and power without the kind of recognition that they are talking about?

ADAKU:
The whole thing sounds too strange to me. These Oyibo people have already caused too much confusion among us. They started selling us. Then they took away our land and said that the only way we could now exist is to write big Oyibo. Our children have acquired their tongue and lost their own. Is that not enough? No! They want it all! They want to carry even the very earth that we walk on. And every day, more and more of our people now speak Oyibo as if that is the only road to life. And the Oyibo empowers them to pile up plenty of paper while the yam barns are empty. Or why do you think we are starving in this country? Because once people can write their name on paper, nothing else matters and it becomes something

shameful to be called a farmer. That is our new disease: Oyibo! And now the head of the family must be turned upside down and men must hand over power to women. Wives must now lie on top of their husbands for women to show power and live a better life? I do not . . . I cannot understand the whole message! I even hear that in Oyibo land now, men marry men and women marry women. . . .

AJAKA:
How?

ADAKU:
Are you asking me? How do I know? Ask the modern ones, who must turn the world upside down for it to stand straight in their eyes! Don't you think all this is getting too much?

AJAKA:
What I really want to know is how they do it!

ADAKU:
Do what?

AJAKA:
I mean men marrying men . . . wonders shall never cease!

ADAKU:
Not with the Oyibo people. . . .

AJAKA:
And women marrying women. . . .

SHERIFAT:
But Idu people have that too; I mean Idegbe. . . .

ADAKU:
But ours is different. Do not confuse the two. Idegbe marries another woman to take her place in the family. HER wife is free to take any man who will give her children to continue the name of the lineage. Then Idegbe can go out and marry her own husband.

SHERIFAT:
But I hear the modern women are arguing that it is still the same.

ADAKU:
How? How can it be the same?

SHERIFAT:
Well, they say it is the same burden for women to promote the interest of the male. My daughter-in-law and I talked extensively about this at home during their last visit.

ADAKU:
Hmn . . . it seems you have forgotten that I too talked with her and her mate . . . I mean her friend on that same occasion. I am still not convinced. In fact, the more I hear you people talk, the more I want

to look inward . . . into our lives to see how this new life is better. I am yet to be convinced. They may be far ahead of us in terms of money. But values . . . especially things to do with the spirit, moral values and the community? Hmm . . . these modern people have yet to show me their humane essence. Money cannot answer all the questions of life and . . . and why we are here. To us, that is important. What is the root of our life . . . here and after?

SHERIFAT:
Yes.

ADAKU:
And that to me is where we part ways from them in our own world.

SHERIFAT:
That is true.

ADAKU:
I've told you people. We must be careful. These new ways will ruin us. . . .

AJAKA:
I know what you mean, our mother.

ADAKU:
If that is what this new power means, let them go and sing that elsewhere and not turn our world, which is already so battered, upside down.

AJAKA:
We wait and see. The women are here. We all discussed it last time they came. Perhaps they will raise that issue again today.

ADAKU:
They dare not. . . .

TOLUE: *(Joining the women.)*
Why don't we wait until our daughters speak to us? We must give them a chance. Daisy is a daughter of Idu and cannot be a stranger to us. She was born, raised and married here. And she is one of us. It is not the same with this other one.

AJAKA:
Why not? Is she not of Idu?

TOLUE:
She is . . . but you know she left home a long time ago.

ADAKU:
I see. Are you then telling me that she is lost to us?

TOLUE:
No! That is not what I am saying. What I mean is that when you have been gone for that long, everything looks different . . . even

strange, and you may have to learn the ways again to enter into that life . . . that world again.

ADAKU:
Then she is a stranger to us?

TOLUE:
Yes! A stranger! That is the best way to put it. She is a stranger here. And . . . and as custom demands, we must be kind and hospitable to our guests. . . .

ADAKU: *(Shouting for everyone to hear.)*
Even when we do not like their ways?

SHERIFAT:
Hmm . . . yes . . . at least we listen to them until they leave. Then we can take the grain and leave the chaff.

ADAKU: *(Impatiently.)*
I am dried of patience now. I cannot wait . . . we have waited long enough. *(Pause.)*
Let our daughter speak to us! Our daughter, speak!

CHORUS OF WOMEN: *(Taking up the chorus.)*
Speak! Speak to us, our daughter! Speak!

ADAKU:
We have been pushed around too long by too many strangers. Now it is time for our own daughter to speak to us. Speak, Adeke!

(General chuckle from the women. ADAKU doesn't quite understand why and shows this by the question etched on her face.)

SHERIFAT: *(Coming to her rescue.)*
Her name is no longer Adeke.

ADAKU:
What?

SHERIFAT:
She changed her name long ago when she left us here.

ADAKU:
So what is she now?

SHERIFAT:
Her new name is "Daasi." . . .

ADAKU:
Hmm . . . Daa-si . . .

SHERIFAT:
That is her new name, Daasi. I too, I'm trying to get used to it.

ADAKU:
Hmm . . . so what is the meaning of this Daasi?

TELL IT TO WOMEN

SHERIFAT:
Who knows?

ADAKU:
Whatever she calls herself.

SHERIFAT:
And now I hear she has that big paper. The one Okafor's son got for which they killed so many cows.

ADAKU:
Which paper? I have no respect for paper. For me, the look of one paper is the same as another.

SHERIFAT:
No! These papers they give them are not the same. There are some papers you get to be able to get other papers. And I hear that the one our daughter has now is the biggest and that the whole of Idu can sit or sleep on it. This is why they now call her "Do-ki-ta."

ADAKU:
True? So that means she can now cure all our diseases? I must show her my ankle that is aching.... (*The women laugh at her again.*)

AJAKA:
No, our mother! Our daughter is not that kind of dokita who cures diseases.

ADAKU:
What kind of do-ki-ta is she, then, if she cannot cure diseases?

AJAKA: (*Laughing.*)
Not all dokita cure diseases, our mother. There are those who do, and those who don't.

ADAKU:
Our daughter should have learnt those skills that will make her cure our diseases instead of learning all that big Oyibo. What kind of do-ki-ta is she, then?

AJAKA:
They say she has the highest paper that can qualify her to work anywhere; even in the "unifersity"!

ADAKU:
Hmm ... I see....

SHERIFAT:
That is why she now works for the president. They pay her bags of money. Don't you see how long the car that brought her is? Is that not enough measure of her success?

ADAKU:
Well, let our daughter speak to us, then! Speak, our daughter.

TELL IT TO WOMEN

(DAISY *takes her place on the platform.* RUTH *steps aside.* YEMOJA *steps down and returns to the crowd.*)

CHORUS OF WOMEN:
Speak to us, our daughter from white man's land! Speak, our own daughter!

DAISY: *(Proudly.)*
My people. Sisters and mothers of Idu! Greetings from the city!

CHORUS OF WOMEN:
Eeih! You are welcome!

DAISY:
This is the great time I have for years longed for and looked forward to. It is my homecoming. It is our day of homecoming in global sisterhood. But most of all, this is your own day . . . not my day! Onto your hands is power reinscribed. (*Pause. By this time, the crowd is becoming restive. And in every corner one can hear rumblings. Despite the microphone,* DAISY *struggles to be heard, and she raises her voice.*)

SHERIFAT: *(Shouting.)*
Order! Let us hear the learned one!

ADAKU:
But that is precisely the point! Can you hear her? (*Turning to all around her.*) Can you understand her? Now, is that not our daughter? Is she not one of us? How then will our daughter, whose umbilical cord was planted right in this soil, come here to speak to us in a borrowed tongue? (ADAKU *is about to rise and challenge* DAISY. SHERIFAT *and other women around her attempt to stop her by holding her down.*)

SHERIFAT: *(To Adaku.)*
Leave her! Let her speak! (*Silence.*) We must learn to handle these modern people. We must handle them with extreme caution, for they are like catfish, slippery and stinging. With your kind of frankness, you may say something now that will annoy them . . . these new breed of women. And then if we do not nod our heads to whatever they say, they will take back what they are going to give us. Leave them! Do not pour sand in our garri.

AJAKA:
And then they will go back to "Gomenti" and report that we are ignorant . . . that we cannot read or appreciate anything.

TOLUE:
Yes! What our mother is saying is right! I saw with my own eyes in

Aboh when they came forward and removed all the pipes they had mounted to give the people water.

SHERIFAT:
These people are like some hot-tempered gods. You do not argue with them, or else they'll take away even the little you had before.

ADAKU:
Let them take, then, and leave us alone. (*ADAKU is rising now to challenge the speaker, but AJAKA inhibits her movement.*)

AJAKA:
But be cautious. . . .

ADAKU: (*Attempting to free herself.*)
Taa, these children! Let it be! Let them go if they must. Why must we be silent because we are going to get what belongs to us? Why? Answer that, you who have lost your pride and now fear your own shadows! What should a ghost mean to an old woman like myself? I will speak! If Nkpordu must fall from the fireside where it is hanging, let it fall and not blame it on the passing wind. I will speak! (*By this time ADAKU is so agitated that she pulls her wrapper together, tightens it on her waist and readjusts her head tie in the typical manner of a woman getting ready for "battle." As this goes on, RUTH becomes uneasy, and DAISY fidgets. DAISY makes a final attempt to reach her audience and slaps the face of the microphone several times.*)

DAISY:
Can you hear me? (*Silence.*) Can you hear me? (*Silence. Faces read other faces around them, and then, as if by general agreement, when DAISY asks again, the women chorus "NO!" ADAKU, springing to her feet immediately after the "NO!" chorus, addresses herself directly to DAISY.*)

ADAKU:
No! We do not hear you! Cannot hear you!

DAISY:
But why? I thought I was loud enough.

ADAKU:
That is not our problem.

DAISY:
What is your problem?

ADAKU:
I will tell you . . . the women will tell. But first, let me ask. It is you, that one they now call "Lu-tu" that I want to answer these questions.

DAISY AND RUTH:
Yes . . .

ADAKU:

> First, I want to know if you are not the same, the one we all gathered in this very village to name as we do all other sons and daughters of Idu eight days after birth?

RUTH:

> Nhnm . . .

ADAKU:

> I am not too old yet that my memory fails me. And I remember what we all named you then. Your father, Mezue, named you Nneka, "mother is supreme." And that too was appropriate, because he had just lost his mother and you were the first child born after that passage. So you were the returning mother. Do you know what that means? I know you don't, but that is another matter that will not be resolved here. And do you still remember the name your mother gave to you? (*Silence.*) I know you don't. Your mother named you Nwanyibuife, "a daughter is a treasure forever." Your grandfather from your mother's side who is related to the mother of my father named you Egonwanne, "you cannot buy a sister or brother, for the blood knot that binds them is priceless." I too on my own part as the Ada of the clan, as well as the sister of your mother's brother, named you Nwa-nne-abuna-oyi, "a sister or brother is not a friend." Why do we say that? Because a friend can come and go, but you are tied to your sister and brother forever . . . in this world and in the next. That is why we cherish that blood. It cannot be sold or bought. It is our view of life. A name is not just a name. It is something . . . it means everything. YOUR NAME IS YOU! So now you call yourself Lu-tu? What does it mean to you? What does it mean to us? What does it mean to your relationship to any of us or to our lives at the time you were born? (*Silence.*) You do not know and do not care to know. So how can you understand how we think? How this world works and what is proper to us for this better life that you say we must have? These are some of the things . . . I . . . we want you to think about and bear in mind as you plan this program you call development for us. You must start from us. We gave you names that spoke of our hearts, of our time and of our world when you were born. I remember your father, Mezue. That great man who came from a great stock of great men and women who have gone to join our mothers and fathers in the other world! They were people of great power and pride, who knew where they came from. Now you have gone out. And you have come back with other names. Not with the names we gave you. You have given yourself another name, or maybe it is the one others have given you. What does Lu-tu mean to

us, or us to Lu-tu? We do not have a blood tie with Lu-tu. But we have one with Nneka. We have one with Nwa-nyi-bui-fe. We have one with Nne-bu-eze. Who are you? Explain yourself and your mission here. Tell us. The women are waiting. Tell us: those people whose name you have taken, did they also take your name in return? I doubt it very much. Without fear of losing my last tooth, tell us, our daughter, who took your name? Or did you give it as a gift to someone there in the new world? Did you give it in exchange for books? And if you took it in exchange for what they offered you, do they know the value of what you gave them? We are waiting. You have so much to tell the women. You must answer these questions before the women can hear you; before you speak to us, your own people, with the corner of your mouth. All we can hear now is everything sounding (*mimicking RUTH*) "psi," "psi" . . . as if you have hot yam in your mouth. Tell us, our daughter. What is so wrong with talking to your people in your own tongue? Why can't you talk to us in the language that we understand? Tell me why you people take pride in going to other people's land, borrow their tongue and then throw your own tongue away? You modern people talk and talk. But I tell you, we do not talk; we speak because we have the word. And that word means power . . . our own power. All people have their own power . . . so why must we abuse our own power or allow others to abuse it? You talk big Oyibo. My people, will all that big Oyibo quench the burning thirst in our throat?

CHORUS OF WOMEN:
NO!

ADAKU:
Will ten baskets full of Oyibo fill the emptiness in our stomachs?

CHORUS OF WOMEN:
NO!

ADAKU:
And now you hear the women. Tell them about their world. Go tell it to women! Tell them what you went to do in the land of the white man. Was it to borrow his wisdom and material to add to our benefit? Give us these good things you brought from the city where they say there is never darkness because men have made stars with hands to blink during the night. This is what my question is. (*Turning to the crowd.*) My people, do I speak your mind?

CHORUS OF WOMEN:
Yes! You do! Well said!! (*Talking drums echo ADAKU's name. This is followed by applause from the women.*)

ADAKU:

Idu, Kwenu!

CHORUS OF WOMEN:

Our mother has spoken! Let them talk! (ADAKU *retreats to her seat. Brief silence.* DAISY *now has the burden of replying to the rural women and their spokeswoman. She begins to address them in an indigenous language that they all understand. But from the way she speaks, it is clear that her initial self-assured confidence and swagger are gone. Her struggles to speak the mother tongue betray such difficulty and are so intermingled with English words and phrases that the rural women equate her language with "Ingili-Igbo," a terrible blend of English and Igbo.*)

TOLUE:

Ingili-Igbo! See the way she chews her mother tongue as if she is chewing hot plantains.

AJAKA:

It's so hot it sticks on the teeth too! (*The women laugh.*)

DAISY: (*Ignoring them.*)

Today is too important for us not to speak with one voice. I "understand you." I am going to accept the "challenge." But first, let me explain myself. I have chosen to speak a foreign tongue not because I want "to despise you," or "alienate you," or make you feel that you are illiterate, but simply because I have come here to act in "many capacities." I am not just a daughter of Idu, I am also married here to this land.

SHERIFAT: (*Interrupting from the audience.*)

Thank you for remembering that you are still our daughter and that you still belong here. You are above all, my wife . . . my son's wife. And may the Earth Goddess guide your feet! (*Everyone looks at* SHERIFAT, *who is not the least embarrassed, and some other women even shout their support to her. After* SHERIFAT's *outburst, everyone quiets down again.*)

DAISY:

I promise . . . promise. It's a promise. This is our era of "Homecoming." This is why we are there, in government to speak for you, to act for you. This is why we are here to bring you the "Good News for Women." Through our persistence, government has approved a new program: "Better Life for Rural Women." This program is meant to bring you comfort, laughter and power. It will bring women to the forefront of "national issues" and give them that power. . . .

CHORUS OF WOMEN: (*Excitedly.*)

Eeih!

ADAKU:

Ahn! That sounds like our daughter!

DAISY:

By this program, women shall have representation in all aspects of government!

CHORUS OF WOMEN: *(Applauding.)*

Eeih!

DAISY: *(Her confidence builds.)*

In particular, government will recognize "the rural woman" who has been held back for years. With the "Better Life Program," government wants to lighten your burden. The rural woman shall have electricity, air conditioner, refrigerator, gas cooker and all the "modern" appliances that lighten the burden of womanhood. *(By this time, the women have become so carried away that they applaud and drum their approval. They break into a short song for her.)*

ADAKU:

Sing for her, Idu! Sing for one who borrowed the white man's tongue and made it better than the creator of the language!

CHORUS OF WOMEN:

Eeih!

ADAKU:

Sing for our great daughter who is our woman-man. Tell me, what can sons do that daughters cannot do?

CHORUS OF WOMEN:

Nothing!

ADAKU:

Sing for our daughters whose feet are so strong they can walk any distance!

CHORUS OF WOMEN:

Eeih! eeih! Our daughters are here!

ADAKU:

Sing for our new women who bring us the best from their sojourn in other lands. *(With each chant, the women now add a chorus: "May the goddess of our land guide their feet." A feeling of euphoria now gets the better of the women. DAISY tries to resume her speech. SHERIFAT helps by calling "Order, order." Silence returns, and DAISY continues her speech.)*

DAISY: *(More assuredly.)*

The key to success in our modern world is edu-ca-tion. EDU-CA-TION! Education for women must be compulsory! Women should prepare for the times ahead. Call for equality with men. Women must know their rights and defend their rights! (*By now, the men whose voices we have been hearing from a safe distance are closer, but the women are oblivious to their nearness. We do not see the men. We only hear them protesting from a near distance.*) Wives, throw away your hoes and take up the pen!

CHORUS OF WOMEN:
Eeih!

SHERIFAT:
Yes! Women too will sign fat paychecks!

DAISY:
Women, you have long been suppressed under the oppressive norms of patriarchy. Redeem yourselves and know that in our modern world, women refuse to be objects of victimization based on the biological factor of their gender. Motherhood cannot be a prerequisite for life!! Women, leave your husbands and go to school! Women, know your lives too can be fulfilled outside motherhood. There is no law making motherhood compulsory. Mothering should be a matter of choice! (*The drums stop abruptly.*)

AJAKA: (*Interrupting.*)
What? (*Silence.*) What did she say?

TOLUE:
That a woman can be something without being a mother.

ADAKU:
Hmm . . . I have a problem with that.

AJAKA:
Me too. But must we accept everything these people say?

TOLUE:
Well, at least now let us nod our heads in agreement.

ADAKU:
Why should we? No! It is shyness that makes someone accept to eat poison!

TOLUE:
At least we can keep them talking. If they offer us that thing they call "salada" which Nebem's daughter-in-law offered her when they took her to Lagos, we will do just like Nebem: take the meat and egg, and throw away the rest. If she should ask you like Nebem's daughter whether you have finished the meal, tell her "yes" instead of risking unnecessary conflict. If she is not satisfied, let her come and examine my shit! (*The women laugh.*) Daughters of my mothers! This Oyibo thing is getting too much for me. I feel as if these people are pumping too much air into my stomach. And you all know me:

my tongue cannot hold back the foamy content of their deceit. I must go now before I say something terrible. And then you all will say that Tolue poured sand into your garri. (*Exit* TOLUE.)

RUTH: (*Helping* DAISY.)

We have come here to open your eyes to make you realize that your lives can be better in many more ways than the ways you have known and accepted. This is why we bring you the "Program on Better Life for Rural Women." This program will soon be launched in the city by the wife of Our President, the champion of women herself. And in preparation, we will require you to choose your representative who will serve as liaison officer between us your representatives on the other side. (*People begin to look around. All eyes turn on* YEMOJA. ADAKU *is first to focus on her, and other eyes follow.* YEMOJA *is being self-conscious and shy.*)

ADAKU: (*Rising.*)

Idu, Kwenu!

CHORUS OF WOMEN:

Eeih!

ADAKU:

You have all heard what the people from the city have to tell to us. They also want us to call our people from inside here who will be our mouth and inner ear before those who are close to "Gomenti." You, daughters of the clan, by tradition are the leaders of others. Wives come after us, but we represent them because they are our wives. It is time for us to retreat and bring back to this gathering our collective choice of who will represent us all. We need a spokeswoman. Idu women, I greet you!!

CHORUS OF WOMEN:

Eeih! (*Umuada, the daughters of the clan, retreat in conference, while the wives of Idu await their decision and return to the gathering. As the oldest daughter of Idu,* ADAKU *has been empowered by the Umuada to report the collective decision of all the women of Idu.*)

ADAKU:

Idu, Kwenu!

CHORUS OF WOMEN:

Eeih!

ADAKU:

The daughters of Idu have met. And I now stand to speak their collective voice. Our choice of leader for the city is one who knows us, and one whom we know. She is one who knows the ways of our land. She is not strange to the ways of the city. She was once in "galama Sukulu." (*Pause.*) Yemoja is our choice! Idu women, do I speak your voice?

CHORUS OF WOMEN:
Eeih! (*The women ululate, drum and chant their approval, but AJAKA has risen to her feet.*)

AJAKA:
Why Yemoja? Why should it be my son's wife who must leave my son and children? Why must it be my own who will wander into the city to be the ears of Idu? I reject your choice! (*This is a surprise to the gathering. Many voices speak at the same time. There is confusion. Sherifat sounds "order" to bring sanity to the group. There is tense silence for a brief moment. Then Yemoja stands up majestically to make a pronouncement.*)

YEMOJA:
I have heard you, mother-in-law. As Ogwashi people say, the ruling Obi has spoken, but it is left to Ogwashi to hear. If the women have chosen me to be their eyes in the city, I, Yemoja, will go to the city. Yes, if the world calls for a new masquerade, I shall be the new masquerade!

AJAKA: (*Alarmed.*)
Obida hear! Is this what a wife, bought here for my son with my own money, has to tell me? (*Silence.*) Yemoja, you have forgotten you are just a wife?

YEMOJA:
I have forgotten nothing. My people gave me to your people as wife, not as slave. A wife is a wife, not a slave! And if the women of Idu make me their choice, I accept to be . . .

AJAKA: (*Screaming.*)
What? Yemoja! (*Silence.*) Are you losing your head before a crowd? (*Silence.*) You have forgotten you are just a wife in Idu? And not even a daughter, who has stronger status? (*Silence.*) Yemoja, think of what you will be losing if you disobey us, your in-laws.

YEMOJA: (*Firmly.*)
These women are my people too. If I am not a daughter in Idu, I am a daughter somewhere else. And that too is important. Remember that! That I am your wife does not mean that I fell from the sky. I too have my roots somewhere. I belong somewhere, sharing the same roots and stronghold with all free sons of Nri. And like you, mother-in-law, I too am somebody's daughter. And like all these Umuada who wield so much power and control in Idu, I too belong to the Umuada of Nri, my own clan. Remember that. If Idu rejects

me as their wife, I am still a daughter somewhere. And my status in Nri is strong, dead or alive!

AJAKA:
Hmm. So this is what it is? If the bird is still in the air and shits ten times, tell me what it will do when it is on the ground? It is sometimes good for the wind to blow so the fowl can show her rump. (*Silence.*) Hmm . . . so this is what the new ways will bring to us; that our wives no longer know their place and grow wings and fly and soar above us? The gods of Idu will not permit it! So you will not hear me, Yemoja?

YEMOJA:
Yes! (*YEMOJA, showing her palms.*) My destiny is here in my palms. No one can take it away. No!! If my Chi, my own personal god who guides me, leads me to the city, I go. Who else but an eternal fool will fight her own god? (*AJAKA can't take the insult any more.*)

AJAKA: (*Rising.*)
The people who married you must hear this! Your people too must hear this! (*AJAKA leaves in anger. The women begin to sing in praise of YEMOJA, who stands, reassured. She walks toward DAISY, whose hands are outstretched to receive her. DAISY shakes hands with YEMOJA while RUTH brings out a gold-plated trophy from her portfolio and solemnly holds it aloft in the manner of a priest as he raises the chalice for all to see. The chants of "YEMOJA" heighten, and YEMOJA stands before her to receive this plaque of honor for her courage and willingness to represent the rural women in this new era.*)

RUTH: (*To YEMOJA.*)
It is my singular honor to present to you this "plague" . . . I mean PLAQUE on behalf of all women. . . .

(*Just as YEMOJA stretches her hand to receive the plaque amidst the excitement and admiration of the women, enter YEMOJA's husband, KOKO, with his mother, AJAKA, followed by the protesting men whose voices have long since been heard in the background. Suddenly KOKO, with fire in his eyes, orders: "Now stop these women!" At first, the excited women are unaware of this intruder. RUTH and DAISY, who are facing the crowd, spot the incursionists from their vantage point before anyone else. KOKO's voice is so high-pitched that the microphone picks it up and magnifies and shatters the sound in the vibrating air. RUTH's hand, outstretched to present the trophy to YEMOJA, freezes in mid-air, while her partner DAISY is alarmed by the appearance of the advancing male crowd. The sudden freeze and silence on the platform spread like an epidemic, causing the crowd of women to turn around and see what those in front of them see in the direction of the words "STOP*

THESE WOMEN." *The air is now charged, for the men have fully arrived at the scene and stand with threatening, disapproving looks directed at one corner of the crowd of women, who by now are standing, too, awaiting the next moment and what it will bring. Silence prevails for a while until* KOKO, YEMOJA's *husband, takes three calculated steps forward toward the center of the crowd. Silence. The eyes of women survey the faces of the angry crowd of male elders before them. Among them are* KOKO's *father,* AJIE, YEMOJA's *father,* OKEKE, *and* TOLUE, *her mother.* TOLUE, *a woman in her early sixties and certainly cast in the traditional mold, is disconcerted at this unwelcome attention. In her nervousness, she tries to adjust the wrapper around her waist, but unfortunately, because of her fidgeting, her hands slip, dropping the wrapper they were meant to tie. This incident provokes laughter among the crowd.* TOLUE *and her family are greatly embarrassed. She departs but soon returns. Then* KOKO *breaks the silence.*)

KOKO: (*Authoritatively.*)
Yemoja, if you are my wife, turn back right now and follow me home! (*Silence. The crowd awaits the next moment.*)

ADAKU: (*Authoritatively, too.*)
And I say no!

AJIE:
What?

ADAKU:
We say no!

AJIE:
Who are the "we"?

CHORUS OF WOMEN:
We are the Umuada, daughters of the clan!! Ajie, head of the clan! We are the beginning and the end. We are the Earth mothers! You need any more introduction? (AJIE *slowly turns around, searching for approving eyes, but the Umuada are poised. And so the two parties stand opposite each other like fowls preparing for a fight. Meanwhile* RUTH *and* DAISY *stand bemused at this turn of events.*)

ADAKU:
Ajie! Begone! And count the gray in your hair. By the time you are done with counting, these women will be on the other side of the river. If you have nothing to do after your counting, take up your hoe and go to farm. Perhaps some sun behind your back bending to earth will bring back memories of honor to you. And if you still seek what else to do, look around you and tell me the faces of those you see. . . .

KOKO: (*Upset by this insult to his father.*)
What has become of you women? You are certainly beginning to

TELL IT TO WOMEN

overreach yourselves. Or maybe you are drunk? (*Pause.*) But it is not for me to take you. That will be left for the elders. . . . I am only here to take my wife.

SHERIFAT: (*Acting like a reporter.*)
Has anyone here taken Koko's wife?

CHORUS OF WOMEN:
No!

ADAKU: (*Mockingly.*)
Brother, is your wife missing? Sisters! My brother's heart is on fire. His wife is missing. Has anyone seen my brother's wife?

CHORUS OF WOMEN:
No!

SHERIFAT:
Brother, you heard the women. No woman here has taken your wife. (*Turning around again to the women.*) Or did any woman take *KOKO's wife*?

CHORUS OF WOMEN:
No!!! The gods forbid it!!!

ADAKU:
Brother. If I were in your position, I would pack my things together and find my way home. (*The women take it up as a chorus.*)

SHERIFAT:
Go home, Koko! BROTHER, GO HOME!

ADAKU:
Put legs together!

SHERIFAT:
Close tight the door!

ADAKU:
And make sure they don't split apart again. . . .

SHERIFAT:
Or fall out of place!

CHORUS OF WOMEN:
Go home, Koko! Brother, go home!! Put your legs together. You're carrying a heavy load. (*The women drum this for a while and then burst into laughter.*)

KOKO: (*Now more aggravated.*)
You women think this is a joking matter? . . . Yemoja is my wife . . . and . . .

ADAKU: (*Interrupting.*)
And what? (*Again to the women.*) Did anyone here say Yemoja is not Koko's wife?

CHORUS OF WOMEN:
> NO! (*AJIE storms into the center and pushes his son aside.*)

AJIE:
> Step aside and let me talk to these women in the only language they understand . . . force!

ADAKU:
> Be careful now. This is our land. We are Umuada. "Ada buisi Ani." We, Umuada, are the head of the land. We, Umuada, are the fingers that look frail but on the day of battle they spark fire. We are Umuada, daughters of the land. . . . Umuada, do I speak your voice?

CHORUS OF WOMEN:
> Eeih! (*The women drum briefly.*)

ADAKU:
> You heard them. The drums have come alive. Who can silence the drums? (*More drums.*) And no matter how important a man, even our own son, thinks he is, his right ends where the right of Umuada begins. His voice ends where the voice of Umuada begins. We are the womb of the earth. From our wombs, sons sprout to earth. From our hands, sons return to earth. It is the life power, the mystery of womanhood. Women are the powers of the earth . . . that no man will ever possess but us. Idu! We are the daughters of the land. This is our gathering!

AJAKA:
> But Yemoja is OUR wife. She is my son's wife and you cannot just take her like that.

ADAKU:
> Ajaka, shut up! Or be fined! Remember now, so long as you are with your husband, you are just a wife, and your role has shifted from that of daughter of the clan to that of wife of the clan. Count your teeth with your tongue. Remember you are talking to us, Umuada, daughters of Idu.

KOKO:
> But our wives are here too.

ADAKU:
> Precisely! (*Turning to the women.*) Are daughters of Idu not wives also?

CHORUS OF WOMEN:
> They are "our wives."

SHERIFAT:
> And people's daughters too.

ADAKU:
> Before they were your wives!

SHERIFAT:
> With rights in their father's homestead even after becoming your wives?

ADAKU:
> With as much right as your daughters.

SHERIFAT:
> Does a daughter cease to be a daughter of Idu because she becomes married to a man?

KOKO:
> Meaning what?

CHORUS OF WOMEN:
> That the difference is clear!

AJIE: *(Assertively.)*
> Meaning that a wife is a wife.

SHERIFAT:
> Meaning that a wife deserves to be treated like a daughter and not something that you possess, reject or crush whenever you will. Why should anyone lose her rights because she becomes a wife?

CHORUS OF WOMEN:
> Why?!

SHERIFAT:
> We know how much you value and respect your mother, Koko. If these women had chosen your mother or daughter would you have come here steaming with anger? *(Silence.)* Brother, answer me! *(KOKO is silent.)* Brother answer me! *(KOKO is still silent.)*

CHORUS OF WOMEN:
> Answer it, brother, answer!

AJIE: *(Overwhelmed.)*
> This is no joking matter anymore. You women are getting out of control. You are becoming more and more reckless. In the name of what? I still do not know. But we must return to the elders who sent us here to protest your gathering. We must end this recklessness!

KOKO: *(Turning to RUTH and DAISY.)*
> You women will be our ruin! You home-wreckers! You ruin the women that you convert to your ways. You uproot them. Women, you ruin everything of value to us! You travel to all these strange lands, import new diseases, infect our women and wreck our homes in the name of what? Transformation? From what to what? We can no longer feed ourselves because women wield the pen. Our children no longer know our customs and traditions because our women live in schools. They learn the customs of others and bury

their own. You betray us to other lands for us to be in perpetual conquest. We are being conquered . . . have always been conquered. Are we the way we were? That is what the women of our land should concern themselves with. Not these foreign ways that take us away. Why don't we convert them to our ways? Why are we always the ones to be converted? Answer me, women! Your grandmothers were great mothers. They were women who held the foundation of our world. But you women of today are nothing but the chaff of mothers! You fake motherhood! You mock motherhood! Where is your pride, women of Idu? It is only us that they conquer. Why don't we conquer too? When the Christians came, they crucified our God and crowned their own. The same with the Moslems. And now our women are embracing a new religion: FE-MI-NISM! Ugh!! Must our women take on the ways of women from other lands to become better women? What do you so-called educated women know? What do you know about custom? What do you know about being women in Idu? How do you know what our women want when you do not even know how to be women yourselves, not to mention our customs? What have you to teach our women? Sometimes I begin to wonder why we send our daughters to school. Why do we send our daughters to school to be ruined?

SHERIFAT: *(Interrupting.)*
You are talking about your daughters. What about your sons?

AJIE:
Those too! I still do not know what we have learned from white man's education in this land.

KOKO:
Ehn! We no longer know ourselves but others. Why can't you see through these people the way we have? But no! You will not! You cannot be anything else but women; only able to see this far from your nose. *(Illustrating with his hand.)*

ADAKU:
Why do you talk like that, Koko?

AJIE:
How else do you want him to talk?

KOKO:
If our wives are adrift, there is a reason for that. A dancer performing by the roadside must have a drummer in a nearby bush. Isn't that what our people say? You and I must know that the drummer is nearby.

AJAKA:
Yes, you are right, my son. *(To AJIE.)* Remember that these are our

TELL IT TO WOMEN

own people. Never lose your bearings and target. And in the process, miss the true enemy. The problem of our world now is these modern women, who think they know it all and infect us with their dangerous ideas. The problem is not the Umuada, for those we know, and they can always speak with one voice. Our problem is these women from the city. Your targets are there! *(She points at DAISY and RUTH.)* The women from the city, not us! Ajie, you are the oldest man in our clan. Umuada know you. You know them. We do not know these women. They will ruin our family.

AJIE:
Ajaka, shut up! Let me speak! You women have always ruined men!

AJAKA: *(Angrily.)*
And what have men always been doing? Making women? Ugh!! Let men be ruined! Let them be ruined if they must and not hold Ajaka, or any women for that matter, responsible for their undoing. And if you should ask Ajaka, Ajaka will say that men deserve very much to be ruined by their own actions, since they are so unreasonable and highhanded! Why not? We'll trade insult for insult! Ajaka is no man's slave to be silenced and intimidated like that. And if anyone should tell me anything that makes my stomach churn again, Ajaka will simply turn her bottom and carry it back home. You husbands think you have the world in your palms! *(Turning to Yemoja.)* And you, Yemoja, you too, do as you please. If you see me in front of your doorstep kneeling to beg you again, poke my eye with a stick . . . or better still, call your dog to chase me out! Go on and walk with your head. Go on, but let no one say Ajaka didn't warn you at this stage. I have done the best I can as your mother-in-law. If you can, pound your fufu inside the mortar; if you can't, pound on the edge of the mortar and crush your flesh along with the fufu too! Count your teeth with your tongue! This new storm from the city will blow over. The city food is now making your mouth water. Beware, my fellow woman! The smell of onion is not the same before and after eating! Remember that! Someday you will remember Ajaka and what she said. And I pray that my ancestors will keep me to hear about this glorious marriage between you and the city women. Ajaka is leaving the stage for you! *(She storms out, and AJIE follows.)*

KOKO: *(Calling AJIE.)*
My father, come back. Let us deal with them or else we will be playing into the hands of these women. Come back! If you must crack the nut of a woman, your hands must be hard and strong. How can you give up so easily? You've forgotten that women are so

easily blown by the wind. They must yield! (*Vehemently.*) Yemoja! (*Silence.*) Yemoja! (*Silence.*) Yemoja! (*Silence.*). Three times I call you. If you know you are my wife, if your community gave you to me and my community as a wife, follow me now or cease to be my wife!

(*Silence. The women await YEMOJA's reaction. YEMOJA stands, wavering. All eyes are now on her. She looks from her husband to the women and from them to the women from the city. Just then, her mother, TOLUE, returns to the stage. With her is YEMOJA's father, OKEKE. Following him is Ajaka, who has gone to invite YEMOJA's parents to drum sense into their child.*)

AJAKA: (*To Okeke.*)
There goes your daughter in the street! Speak to her if you still know her, . . . if she still understands your language. Above all, tell her that she is somebody's wife just in case she has forgotten. (*Mocking laughter from the women.*)

OKEKE:
No! No, women! Suspend laughter! This matter is urgent and serious!

SHERIFAT:
Is there now a decree against laughter?

OKEKE:
I don't know any reasonable man who goes chasing after a rat when his house is on fire!

ADAKU: (*Laughing.*)
Ohooo! So your house is on fire? Who set the house on fire?

OKEKE:
Women!

CHORUS OF WOMEN:
Hmm . . .

OKEKE:
What else is there to say? They tell you the house is on fire and you are asking if Baba's beard is burning in it too? You women are impossible! Ugh! Sometimes I wonder if it is the same god that created man that also created woman.

CHORUS OF WOMEN:
We wonder about that too! (*Silence.*)

OKEKE:
You women are an impossible breed! And you make me wonder if you truly belong to this land! (*Pause.*) But that is another matter. . . . For now, we must face the matter at hand. (*He turns to YEMOJA. Brief*

silence.) Hmm . . . Eneke nti nkpo! Eneke the deaf one! Where do they say you are going? *(Silence.)* Where do they say you are going? And leaving your husband and children? In the name of what? *(Silence.)* I can now see that you are not only deaf, you are dumb too! *(He turns around in anger to* YEMOJA's *mother.)* That is your daughter! Speak to her! Speak to her if you still know her! Speak to her, you women who do not know your daughters and cannot prepare them for proper leaving in the world! Speak to your daughter. My family will not be ruined by you women whose ears are planted behind their heads! Go and tell her that, you mothers of waste, who fail to tell your children what best they need to know!

TOLUE:

Enough! Enough, Okeke! No! That is enough! Enough! Hold your tongue! Did you come here to lay my bottom bare before the world or did you come here to retrieve your daughter?

OKEKE:

I have not come here to lay anyone bare. I only speak the truth.

TOLUE:

Then hold your truth, Okeke! Hold it! Nobody needs that bitterness now! Hold it! And note no woman has come here to take lessons . . . least of all, take lessons from men about how we must raise our daughters! *(Silence.)*

OKEKE: *(Interrupting, pushing his wife aside.)*

When will women know the time for petty quarrels? This is no time for it! So step aside and let me handle this matter. You are too fickle-minded. You women can go eat each other after this event. For now, my daughter is the issue. Leave Yemoja to me. *(Pause. His mood changes. He talks more persuasively now.)* Yemoja is my daughter. And I am her father. *(*OKEKE *takes a look at the crowd.)* Why don't you all leave us alone now?

CHORUS OF WOMEN: *(Protesting.)*

We want to hear it! Tell it here! We must hear now! We must hear now! Speak to her here!

OKEKE:

Why?

CHORUS OF WOMEN:

What concerns one concerns all.

OKEKE:

Why should I? Yemoja is my daughter. And I am her father! She is my own Yemoja, named after my own mother, who crossed the River Niger all the way from Yorubaland in the West to bear her for my father in Igboland. That child you see is the jewel of my family. What do you think Yemoja means to me and my world?

ADAKU:

Yemoja is Onokwu, Goddess of the Sea in our world.

OKEKE:

Ohho! So you know? So you women know who Yemoja is? Why then do you want to burn the land? Tell me women, WHY DO YOU WANT TO TURN THE SEA AGAINST THE LAND?

ADAKU:

Yemoja is us! We are Yemoja! Yemoja is not just Yemoja!

OKEKE:

Are you women trying to turn my daughter into something other than herself?

CHORUS OF WOMEN:

She is our representative! Yemoja is us! Yemoja is every woman here!

ADAKU: *(Chant-like.)*

She is a daughter!

CHORUS OF WOMEN:

She is a wife!

SHERIFAT: *(Chanting.)*

She is a mother!

CHORUS OF WOMEN:

Yemoja is us! *(Deafening sounds of the drum. The women form a circle.)*

ADAKU:

Yemoja, stand! Stand and let all women see!

CHORUS OF WOMEN: *(Chanting.)*

Yemoja! Yemoja! Yemoja! *(SHERIFAT hits the drum.)*

SHERIFAT:

Order!! *(Silence returns to the crowd.)* Order. Yemoja will break her silence! *(The drums calm down. YEMOJA prepares to speak and walks toward the center of the circle. Drums greet her, intoning her name.)*

ADAKU:

Speak to us!

OKEKE:

Yemoja, denounce these women!

ADAKU:

Yemoja! The women are waiting. Speak to us!

OKEKE:

Yemoja, hear your father!

ADAKU:

Yemoja, hear the women!

CHORUS OF WOMEN: (*Drumming.*)

Speak to us! Yemoja! Yemoja! Tell us! Tell it to women!

OKEKE:

Women, won't you leave my family alone?

CHORUS OF WOMEN:

Yemoja! Yemoja! Tell us! Tell it to women!

OKEKE:

This is ridiculous! Women, what do you want to hear? Women, what do you want? That my daughter should be your ritual sacrifice? Women, leave my family alone. Is there no room for privacy anymore? Leave me alone! Idu! Leave my daughter alone! Leave my family alone! Idu! Where is the family gone?

ADAKU:

Here! (*The women laugh.*)

CHORUS OF WOMEN: (*Drumming.*)

Yemoja! Yemoja! Yemoja!

OKEKE: (*Turning to* YEMOJA.)

And Yemoja? You, my daughter, won't you stop the women? (*Silence.*)

CHORUS OF WOMEN: (*Drumming.*)

Yemoja! Yemoja! Yemoja!

OKEKE: (*Resignedly.*)

Well, my daughter has sold me . . . sold me to women! There is nothing else to say. Women, go on and drum! My own daughter has broken my arms and handed the drums over to you. Women, go on! Go on! Go on and drum! Who do I blame but my daughter, who decides to show my nakedness before the world and the eyes of these mocking women? No! Okeke has no one to blame but his daughter, who sold her own father for nothing . . . or at best, for the promise of a better life! What that better life is, Okeke cannot tell. What is this better life? Women, you have the word! My throat is dried of words. Women, may your will be done. I am done. The stage is now yours. Drum! Go on and drum!! (*The atmosphere is now charged as* YEMOJA *stands against her father before the women acclaiming* YEMOJA.) Yemoja! Yemoja! Yemoja! Three times I call you. If you are my daughter, if you call me your father, say goodbye to the city women. Renounce all the promises and offerings. And stay to be the pillar of our home and tradition. Can you, knowing all the landmarks, allow yourself to roam the fields? You will let yourself play with the bloody beaks of these city hawks? *(Silence.)* Yemoja! It is from my household, I, Odogwu, the keeper of our land and its treasures. How can it be said I donated my daughter as instrument to ruin the family, the very root of Idu? How, Yemoja answer me? *(Meanwhile, TOLUE, YEMOJA's mother, is becoming very restless and anxious. She makes signs and looks imploringly at her daughter, praying that she will change her mind and renounce her commitment to the women. Silence.)*

YEMOJA: *(Finally breaking her silence.)*
Why has it become so important to you now that I am your daughter? Was I also not your daughter when you chose not to send me to the university? And preferred instead to educate my brother? What does it matter now to anyone what I do? Yemoja is just a girl who will only grow to become a wife in Idu. So why should anybody care that the reed is broken in the tide? *(Silence.)* Did you not hurry me into marriage to be able to train my brother? *(Silence. Between the silences, YEMOJA turns to KOKO.)* And you, what have you done with me? Am I not your NOTHING? Am I not the rag for wiping your hands and feet? *(Silence. KOKO and OKEKE look at YEMOJA in absolute bewilderment.)* You have made me a nothing. Kept me as nothing. Now, for once . . . once in a lifetime, I choose, I choose to do something with myself. I choose to reclaim my life. I choose to be in line with the women of the world. What else is a woman to do? Where else is she to run? Must she beg the earth to yawn and swallow her up? No, father! No, husband! Father, I love you! Husband, I love you! But I am not you . . . and you are not me. I too am different; with eyes to look the world in the face and confront it if I can. You need the space, I need the space to see life in its fullness. You have your destiny. I have mine. My destiny is here in my palms, and I know now that I too can claim it and hold it! I want to become something for me, my own sake, not for what you or anyone else wants me to be. Why must I first be your wife before I am myself? Why must I be my father's daughter before I am myself? Why must . . . why must I be someone's mother before I can be myself? Why can't I be me? Eh, Koko? Why can't I be me? Koko, answer me? *(Silence reigns.)* Does anyone ever think of me? Me as me? Why must a female always be someone's wife and daughter and mother before she can gain recognition in the eyes of the world? *(Silence.)* Idu! Idu! Why can't you let me be? Let me be ME! Idu, I too have a voice! Hear me too!!

CHORUS OF WOMEN: *(Intoning with the drum.)*
Idu, let her be! Let her be! Be, Yemoja! Yemoja! Yemoja!

TELL IT TO WOMEN

ADAKU:
>Be, Yemoja!

CHORUS OF WOMEN:
>Be, Yemoja! Be, Yemoja! Be, Yemoja!

OKEKE: (*Again persuasively.*)
>I can now see who the problem is. The problem is not my daughter, but women. I can see. (*Silence.*) It is not my daughter: it is women. Yemoja! I can see these women have taken your sight. You are getting lost in the wilderness. Retrace your steps now . . . now that we are still here to give you support. . . .

YEMOJA: (*Irritably.*)
>I need no support! I can stand on my own! That is what these city women have to tell. That is the language of the new world. We cannot be deaf to it. We must hear it! The women must hear it! The women must tell it!

OKEKE:
>I see . . . you are not only lost, you are drunk too. Where is a man to begin to salvage a lost daughter and a senseless horde of women? Yemoja, no matter what you are and hope to become, remember I am your father and you will always be mine. If women from the city have come to feed you with tasty poison, I see through it, Yemoja. You are my daughter. Yemoja, hear me! Yemoja, think! Think! This is the time! Think again!

YEMOJA:
>And that is what I am doing now . . . thinking . . . thinking. I am thinking again. If you valued me so much, why did you not send me to school as you did my brother? (*YEMOJA's mother, no longer able to keep her peace, steps forward.*)

TOLUE:
>Let me answer her.

OKEKE: (*Aside to TOLUE.*)
>No! Let me answer her! We are walking on very slippery ground. Child, you do not know. But it is our duty . . . of us mothers and fathers to tell. Otherwise, how will the young ones know their bearings if they do not know where we and they are coming from? This is why we must tell. (*He pauses and then smiles.*) Yes, daughter! We sent the men first to school to learn the white man's ways just the way we send them to hunt in the forest to bring back the goods to add to our riches. We do not lead our daughters onto shores we are not sure of. Why? Because daughters are the eternal treasures of our land. It is like giving away the self . . . the earth, the land, and your

entire being. How can we risk our treasures that way? No! My jewel! My mother! Have you forgotten you are my mother come back to life? Nne-bu-eze! Mother is king! Mother is supreme! And when someone kills another, by tradition that lost soul must be replaced. But we do not send our male to that family in payment. We send our female child to reproduce their kind in that family. The family of one killed will not accept a male issue. To them, the male is like a rooster that is bred for food. A rooster is not like a hen, which can create and recreate. A hen has more lasting value. In the same way too we send our sons to hunt in the forest, not our daughters. It is sons that go hunting for treasures. And then they return home to bring back goods that nurture our lineage. Our daughters have always been, and will always be, our pride. How then can we become the eye that mocks its own face? (*Silence.*)

YEMOJA:

I too want to be the hunter of values with my brother! I too seek to bring back new treasures. How can I always remain here to receive from the hands of my brother? I too have my hands and can fetch the world out there!

OKEKE:

So, Yemoja, you will not hear! You will not hear! Not even the voice of your father? If I, Okeke, Odogwu, huge hands that wrestle the earth, I, Diji, master farmer and owner of the biggest yams in Idu—if I am your father, for the last time I tell you, renounce these new women and their offerings! (*Silence, tension.* OKEKE *turns to his wife.*) You better speak to your daughter now, because once I make up my mind, nothing will ever turn me away from my course!

TOLUE: (*Imploringly.*)

Yemoja. The whole land awaits your voice. Yemoja, save us! Save our faces! Save our land! Save the family! Save the man! Save the children! Save! Save, Yemoja! Save! Save the land! (*Silence.*)

KOKO:

Yemoja, for the last time, if you cannot hear my words as your husband, and words from your father fall and bounce back from the stony walls of your ears, for the last time you have a chance. Obey now what we urge you to do, or from now on cease to be my wife and return to your father! (YEMOJA *looks from one face to another.*)

OKEKE:

No! Not my house! There is no place in Okeke's house for one whose ears are lost to the wind! (TOLUE, *anguished, holds up her right breast to the sun and chants ritualistically.*)

TELL IT TO WOMEN

TOLUE:
You gods of Idu! Ancestors, hear me! Unplug these rocks from the deaf ears of my daughter! Yemoja! Yemoja, hear me! Renounce the new women and return home!! (*Silence. There is tension everywhere.*)

YEMOJA: (*Gracefully, solemnly.*)
Father, you can't stop the sun rising. Mother, you can't stop the milk teeth from falling when adult teeth press for vision. Husband, you can't stop the young buds shooting out from the chests of females flowering. How can you? No, you can't! Father, I will understand. Mother, I will understand. Husband, I will understand. I am not a child anymore. I am a grown woman. But I want to move with the world. If all else goes, let me go with the world. If all else comes, let me come with the world. I want to go and come. And not be there standing still while the world around me is in rapid motion. I too want to move . . . move with my eyes! The principle of life is to give and take! Let me "give"; let me "take" from the world around me. Rarely does the water of life flow in a communal barrel. This is my own barrel: each one with his or her barrel. This one is mine. If I break it along the path, do not worry. There will always be another water barrel. There will always be another road to life. Why must I be afraid to set out when I know that all there is in life is the journey? I am ready. Let me go! But I love the family and want to remain an integral part of the circle. How can we make the circle if we cannot go and come? That is the course of life: going and coming until the circle is complete. But I too must chart my own course in the circle. As faces of husbands, mothers and fathers change in the sun, so does the moon. I want to see from all sides. I have seen the world from your side. Why can't you see it from my side? I have made my choice. If, when I return, my father tells me there is no place for me in his homestead, I shall understand. If I return and my husband tells me there is no place for me on his bed, I shall understand. But for now, let me go . . . let me go . . . I must go! The women have waited enough. . . . (*YEMOJA walks toward RUTH to accept the plaque.*)

CHORUS OF WOMEN: (*Breaking into hilarious song.*)
Yemoja! Yemoja!

OKEKE: (*Turning back.*)
I have said it time and time again. It is no use trying to understand women! (*Turning to KOKO and his family.*) My in-laws, I must see you later to resolve this matter. (*As the women sing and drum for YEMOJA, they "spray" her with money and gifts of clothes as if she were a ritual celebrant.*)

ADAKU: *(Decking YEMOJA's neck with beads.)*
Here, our daughter! Our jewel! Take nzu, this white clay, for luck on your long road to life. Take, and go well . . . for you . . . for us. Go! Be our mouths! Be our ears! Be our eyes to see the new world! It is you we know. Yemoja! Yemoja! Yemoja! Go! Sail "Assia," the beauty of rivers! Sail, Onokwu-Yemoja, Goddess of the Sea! The city calls! Sail!! Sail to the city! Sail and bring back to us the sea's treasures of corals. Sail and bring us precious gems and stones! Sail, Yemoja! Sail, our handmaid of the sea! Go! To the city, craft our course! Prepare our path! Tell the city women we are coming! We are coming! Go tell it to women!!!

CHORUS OF WOMEN: *(Chanting and drumming.)*
Yemoja! Yemoja! Go!! Go! Tell it to women! Go! Tell it to women! Tell it to women! Go! Go! Go! Yemoja! Yemoja! Yemoja! *(DAISY now stands to address the women.)*

DAISY:
Well said, women. Yemoja is now in our hands. We understand and will use her very well. While we await your coming, Yemoja will stay with us in the city. She will live in my household to learn new steps for the better life. As you may know, the key to life in the new world is productivity . . . self-reliance for selfhood. Each fights her own course. That should not be too difficult to imagine. So be prepared.

RUTH:
In the new world, nothing goes for nothing. Experience, as they say, is the best teacher, and Yemoja will learn and bring back the knowledge to enrich your world. But note, she will render services to us for which she will be paid. Yemoja now belongs to us . . . she is one of us. So sisters, be ready. We will teach her, and she in turn will teach you. Thank you, sisters! We await your coming!

(DAISY hands RUTH the gold-plated plaque, which she presents to YEMOJA. The women drum in excitement . . .) *(. . . The phone rings. Yemoja is startled and screams.)*

YEMOJA: *(Waking from her dream.)*
Mother, I'm here. *(Pause.)* Where are you? Where am I? *(She jumps to her feet. She is dazed, wondering and asking.)* Where are the women? *(Echoes follow her questions. The phone rings again and again. She walks toward it, nervously begins to pick it up but changes her mind.)* What am I to do now? The phone rings, I cannot pick it up. All the grunting I've heard here since I came to this cell is: "Don't . . . don't. Don't! Don't piss in my toilet! Don't. Don't touch my food! Don't! Don't! Don't!" They treat me like a pig. They say my

accent is too heavy when I answer the phone. They say my manners are crude and I'm a disgrace to womanhood. That is dirt splashed on my face by my fellow women. Who knows when the man will start his own abuse? So far the man has not bothered with me. He says he's working . . . working . . . executive meetings here and there. He's here and everywhere. Hmn . . . city people? Ugh! Who knows when these city people ever have time to enjoy the money they pursue everywhere? And their women shouting like flies on top of excrement. *(Pause.)* And yet I followed them because I thought they believed in their words about sisterhood. Who am I to trust? They say they can't risk losing face from their friends . . . important callers. Big . . . big . . . people . . . governors, ministers, professors. Even the president calls her at home. And she's upstairs now . . . she and that "busybody" they call Ruth. "Busybody die for gutter!" Hmn . . . what modern women do? *(Pause.)* When the man is away, they lock themselves up . . . and they say they're working . . . working on each other? Eh! Only our ancestors know what work modern women do together behind closed doors! And on the door there's a sign: DO NOT DISTURB. What is a woman "disturbing" another woman for? May the devil bend their waists, these people who subvert roles nature assigned to them! May the gods wet their faces with piss! *(Pause.)* I'm going to show them! I'll show them that Yemoja is a true daughter of Nri and not a slave born. I will . . . I will. . . . *(The phone begins to ring again.)* Oh, these people! (YEMOJA, *again confused, runs to the phone, touches it, and changes her mind about picking it up until it rings again. She tries to adjust her voice to sound like her elite boss.)* Hiilooo? *(Pause.)* Hilooo? May . . . may . . . I know who's calling? Pleeeaase? *(Pause.* YEMOJA's *confidence is growing now.)* Minister? *(Alarmed.)* The Minister for Home Affairs? Okay, Sirr! Hold on, Siir. . . . Yes, Siiirrr! Yes, Siirr! Medem is home. *(She drops the phone, runs to the upstairs bedroom, and knocks on the door rather feebly.)* Medem! Medem! *(Silence.)* Medem, phone!

DAISY: *(Screaming from inside.)*

What? Your mother! Go and swallow that phone, bitch!

YEMOJA:

It's . . . it's phone. . . . *(Pause.* YEMOJA *again confused. Does she return to the phone and announce to the minister that madam is unwilling to answer? Or again try to call madam's attention to the importance of her caller? She decides on the latter and knocks at the door, this time more audibly.)* Ma . . . madam. It's the . . .

DAISY: *(From inside.)*

The what? Can't you people ever take simple instructions? Is your head so thick that you can't remember anything? Haven't I told you never to wake me up in my sleep? (*DAISY now appears outside the bedroom door, blasting YEMOJA and trying to put on her housecoat over her lingerie. DAISY shows YEMOJA the sign on the door.*) And if you suffer from such intense amnesia, can't you read the sign on the door? "DO NOT DISTURB!" Okay? (*Silence.*) Now, carry your dirty stinking dead body off my doorstep!

YEMOJA:
But medem . . .

DAISY: (*Flying off at her again.*)
What are you butting? These people . . . always having one "but" after another! Can't you let a woman rest?

YEMOJA: (*More firmly.*)
The minister . . .

DAISY: (*Flying down the stairs, RUTH following behind her.*)
The minister is on the line and you're standing there eating your words like you are eating hot yams? (*Sighing.*) These people! (*Pause.*) Now, minister for what?

YEMOJA:
For Home Affairs . . .

DAISY: (*Running to the telephone.*)
My god! These people will ruin me! (*DAISY now takes to her heels to catch the phone before the minister hangs up.*)

RUTH: (*To YEMOJA.*)
Why didn't you say so all this time?

YEMOJA:
But . . . but . . .

RUTH:
But what? Idiot. . . .

YEMOJA: (*Angered.*)
She won't let me speak. . . .

RUTH: (*Haughtily.*)
As if you had something of worth to say? Get the hell out of my sight! (*Exit YEMOJA, sulking.*)

DAISY: (*Running down the stairs, cursing.*)
Don't mind the bitch! (*Mocking YEMOJA's accent.*) "She won't let me speak"! Shoot!

RUTH: (*Returning to the bedroom.*)
These rural women—always scapegoating . . . always blaming their failings on someone. Always! Always. . . . Someone must be responsible for their failings. And this is their local champion? Yaaack! Can't stand her! I pity Daisy. I can't stay under the same roof with

her for one day . . . not even one day! Shooot! Useless crowd. I told you. The government is wasting time and money. Useless!

DAISY: *(She grabs the phone.)*
Hi dear! Pardon the delay. You know these maids . . . necessary evil . . . crude spill-over straight from hell. . . . Yes. . . . Yes . . . I got a new one from Idu. . . . Oh, she must be thirty-one years old. But you know. These backward village women are babies. Baby factories too. Pastime, tending the baby factory. . . . Yeah. . . . Every sex act must produce at least one baby. . . . Pleasure? Ugh! Forget sexual pleasure where these women are concerned! Even dogs on the street place more value on the act than these rural robbers. . . . Oh yes! Highway robbers are even better than these city maids . . . pickpockets. Pickpockets steal your money. . . . Your lover? Can't risk that. You kidding? Rural women make better maids. . . . Yes. . . . I know. . . . They are dense, thick-headed, but much easier to manage. . . . You know: like clay? Yes . . . you bet. . . . Their brains? That's if they have any. . . . Like tabula rasa . . . brand new slate to write on. And you score 100 percent credit for it. Oh, rural women? They're so receptive and appreciative to new ideas . . . learned ideas! Anything is welcome. A flash of light in their state of darkness? Certainly. . . . And they adore you . . . anyone with enlightened ideas. . . . Worship? Oh, you should have seen them worship me at the village . . . me and Ruth. . . . We're their "sheroes"! Yeeess! . . . You should have seen husbands and fathers shaking. And the women were like little children who had wandered into some orchard with plenty of fruit. They just gobbled up everything! Hmmm . . . well, we got the magic. The new messiahs! Sure! What did you expect? We're the angels sent from on high to rescue them. That's how come they gave me this woman to serve. . . . Yes. . . . The new maid. Hmm . . . she's here as their representative. . . . Yes . . . everything is set. The date is now fixed? When? The last day in August? Whao!! Too near. Why? I doubt if we're ready for them yet. But we don't tell them that though. . . . So why choose such a close date? Ohoooh! To coincide with their new yam festival! That's smart! Smart! You got it! I got it! Their communal celebration of harvest, the new year . . . the farming season will be over. The harvest! . . . plenty, plenty of yams . . . and other crops. . . . Plenty of produce to show the world. Yes! The rural women can then show off their produce to the whole world at the launching. . . . This is the better life . . . yeah! Or how else are we going to convince or justify the huge sums we are making the government invest in this program? And Ruth's research too! Yes! Her promotion to full Professor of Feminist Studies hangs on

the success of this program. . . . Yes! You remember she got a huge grant to undertake this program on the Better Life for Rural Women? . . . Yes . . . it was her idea to begin with . . . that's why it's more important to her than any of us. . . . Our mutual interest? You know now? . . . Yes. . . . For those of us in government. Yes! We'll make some cool money, of course! Yes . . . yes . . . international fame. Yes . . . of course, bringing ourselves to world attention . . . feminism is the fashion . . . the new vogue now. Yes . . . fulfilling the requirements of the UN Declaration of the Decade for Women. Yes . . . the government too wants attention and votes for the next election. Yes, buy the people . . . buy up their conscience. What else? Well who cares what happens afterward? Who cares what happens to the program after the election? My own money will be resting in some Swiss bank, of course! *(Laughter.)* But I know your account in Switzerland is breathing . . . hmm . . . heavily too! I also know that Ruth will get her promotion on this rural women program. . . . Yes . . . we're no fools. . . . And neither is the government. . . . Yes. . . . What did you say? The government has approved how much for the program? TEEENNNNN MILLIOOOOONNNN! Whao! *(DAISY becomes hysterical and begins calling RUTH.)* Million! RUUUUTH-HHH! My God! Ten million! TEN MILLION! MY GOD! Wao!! Bravo! Hurrah for women!! Salute to feminism! Victory for women! Victory for sheroes!! *(RUTH "flies in" to share in whatever victory her partner is celebrating as DAISY drops the phone.)* TEN MILLION! TEN MILLION! Yemoja, bring that case of champagne! *(Silence.)* Yemoja! *(Silence.)* Yemoja! Where is she?

RUTH: *(Getting impatient, takes up the bell on the table.)*
Ring the bell for the idiot. Why waste your energy and time calling her? The security guard's number is one, the gardener two. What's Yemoja's identification number?

DAISY:
Three.

RUTH:
Yeah, three times then. Strike the bell, and soon you'll see her running here like a mad dog. . . . *(RUTH rings the bell for YEMOJA. YEMOJA is not yet in sight. RUTH rings the bell again, but YEMOJA is not forthcoming. They stare at each other, wondering where she might have gone. Silence. DAISY takes the bell from RUTH and begins to ring it impatiently. While she does that, RUTH goes over to the refrigerator in the kitchen to fetch a drink, which she pours out for herself and for DAISY. RUTH sighs.)* Well, darling, while waiting for the snails, let's celebrate us. . . .

DAISY:
>What else is there to do? We celebrate ourselves! *(She drinks and sighs.)* Yeah! these rural women are something else!

RUTH:
>They got some of the most simplistic minds you'll ever come across....

DAISY:
>They're just like a herd of cattle.... Ugh, these uneducated women living in gangs they call communities!

RUTH:
>It's incredible how foolish village women are! They see marriage as the only means of social mobility.

DAISY:
>And that also applies even to the quarter-baked literate ones among them. These backward women flock in their thousands to the marriage altar lured by the sweetness of the wine.

RUTH:
>Oh, the intoxicating effect of new wine? Sweet ... sweet.... Marriage and social mobility my foot!

DAISY:
>You soar, get drowsy and dizzy.

RUTH:
>But it soon clears. And you're left to endure the flat stale taste of alcohol....

DAISY:
>Oh, Ruth! You hit the truth right there on the head! *(Pause. She sighs.)* And you, my Ruth, were smart never to have subjected yourself to marriage. Marriage is the greatest sentence any woman could ever impose on herself.

RUTH:
>I tell you, dear, marriage is an unforgivable insult to women. And I see no reason why any educated woman with her head still sitting on her shoulders should give it any thought, much less accept it. I'm sorry, darling, but that's the way I see it. You should never have married Okei! *(Pause.)* And the love faded away a long time ago. Now you're trapped and sentiment's getting into it because of children. Husbands and children? Ugh! I couldn't deal with all that shit and aggravation. I could never mortgage my life, my independence for nobody! Nobody! Not even for my own mother! And I don't owe anyone any obligation ... well ... darling, I know what you're going to say ... your usual arguments. No, darling. I love you very much, but I too am entitled to my opinion. No apologies!!! *(Brief silence.)*

DAISY:
> Yeah! They say love is blind.

RUTH:
> Until marriage opens your eyes! *(They laugh.)*

DAISY:
> Now I can see . . . I am a first-hand witness. I can see now. . . .

RUTH: *(Emphatically.)*
> CLEARLY! *(They chuckle, holding each other's hands. A car pulls up. DAISY pulls RUTH toward the window to peep through it with her.)*

DAISY:
> I wonder who that is. *(They listen.)* Maybe it is Okei.

RUTH:
> You women must have special antennae for sniffing husbands. . . .

DAISY:
> And where is Yemoja? Why is it taking that snail so long to come and tell me who the hell is out there? *(They hear the sound of the car speeding off again.)*

RUTH:
> You don't think it's Okei anymore?

DAISY:
> Well, I could swear it was the sound of his car, but . . . *(Pause.)* Strange. . . .

RUTH:
> Why do you think he would drive in that way and speed off again without entering his own house?

DAISY:
> Well, who knows? *(Pause.)* He's not dumb anyway. And he knows I don't really care about him anymore. He may be suspicious, reading between the lines of our relationship, and maybe getting jealous also.

RUTH:
> But why should he be jealous? Things haven't been working out between you and him for a long time. So why is he jealous? Love cannot be forced! It's a question of individual choice. Well, I hope your husband has heard the words: "individual rights, liberty and freedom." If his education hasn't led him yet to appreciate the philosophy, I should be more than willing . . . indeed I would be most delighted to give him a lesson or two on my own account. *(Silence.)*

DAISY:
> It takes time for people to accept . . . get used to new ideas . . . and

especially such radically unconventional ones as mine and yours. That takes time for people to digest.

RUTH:
I see, but I cannot be convinced. *(Pause.)* Where exactly did Okei go?

DAISY:
Who knows where husbands go exactly? All I can tell you is that he said he was going to the village.

RUTH:
He's rather frequently in the village nowadays. What's the attraction there? Are you sure he's not up to something fishy?

DAISY:
How's Daisy to know? I don't belong there. They could be arranging a new wife for him for all I care. Shoot!

RUTH:
It may very well be.

DAISY:
Who cares? That will give me the license . . . the impetus that I need to make a clean break and make ours public.

RUTH:
You really think you need anybody's license or approval to do that?

DAISY:
At least, the moral justification. . . .

RUTH:
Darling, just stop! I love you very much, but I see we can never agree on some of these issues. I live my life the way I want to. Nobody runs it for me! It doesn't matter to me what people think. . . .

DAISY: *(Calmly.)*
Well, dear. That too is important. I mean we may have all we desire from life, but I also think it's important how we live it, how people perceive us. I mean, no matter how much power one has, no one lives in a vacuum. . . .

RUTH:
Oh, dear! We better change the subject. I'd hate to have a confrontation with you of all people. If you think like them I wonder who else could be on my side to campaign against homophobia.

DAISY:
True, we agree on many things. But don't let's lose sight of who we are and where we are coming from. We're Africans, and you know precisely what children, fatherhood, and motherhood especially mean to the people: male and female. For these people, children,

fatherhood and motherhood have spiritual, metaphysical significance for continuity. You know their cyclic view of the world here and hereafter? That is the core . . . the basis of their life cycle. . . .

RUTH: *(Violently.)*

NO, Daisy! NO! Not you! *(Silence.)* I can't believe that you too could be thinking like these people. NO! *(Pause.)* I feel abandoned and alone.

DAISY:

I don't see why you should feel that way . . . just because we disagree on one minor point and detail about life. It's okay. There should be room for growth. I'm trying to get used to the idea. Just give me time.

RUTH: *(Sighing.)*

I'm getting quite disappointed in you. You're too slow for me.

DAISY:

Be patient. I . . . we'll get there. *(Pause. She goes over to RUTH and kisses her.)* Darling. I promise . . . we gonna make it . . . together . . . we gonna make it. Cross my heart. I'll be with you till the end. *(Silence. DAISY pours out more wine. They drink. The phone rings. DAISY picks it up.)* Hello? Hello? Hello? *(She drops the phone angrily and sighs.)* What the hell is going on in this house? Nothing seems to be going right here anymore. So many unsolved mysteries . . .

RUTH:

My guess is that your husband is checking up on you.

DAISY:

Let him go and fuck himself . . . excuse the language. Am I his slave?

RUTH:

He's often traveling to his village nowadays. Why?

DAISY:

Well, I know you'll hate to hear this, but I've heard him tell his friends that he's too far from his culture and wants to keep quite close to it. He argues that the experience of schooling abroad was quite alienating and now he works so far away from home in the city. It's a way of bridging the gap between the rural and urban. . . .

RUTH:

Let the bridge collapse! *(Pause.)* But if you really ask me, I think your husband is arranging something . . . something that's going to affect you . . . or even change your life completely. And they can make voodoo on you too to tie you down. I don't trust these villagers.

DAISY:

I hope it doesn't happen, but let's wait and see. Maybe they're just trying to arrange a new wife for him, and that would suit me just fine. I may be just stating the obvious. Okei might be searching. . . .

RUTH:
Who cares really? What else could he be searching for? He has you. He wields a lot of power in government. He's Secretary to Government. What else does a man want? What else?

DAISY:
His mother's breast perhaps! *(They laugh.)* We're laughing, but that is true. Okei might just be like any other man I know: searching . . . searching . . . always searching for some breast or another. . . .

RUTH:
Especially for their mother's breasts . . . you know what I mean?

DAISY:
Sure! Sure! I too am coming to that conclusion.

RUTH:
What precisely?

DAISY:
Hmm . . . that men are addicted to their mother's breasts. And once they lose them, they're still not actually weaned. They go in search of replacements. You know what I mean? Surrogates . . . you know, like pacifiers and bottle teaties? *(They laugh.)* I'm certain men don't really need wives but mothers. That's why they get so easily disappointed in their women, because they're looking for mothers and they get wives instead!

RUTH: *(Laughing.)*
So what you're saying then is that men marry wives as surrogate mothers? *(They laugh.)*

DAISY:
It might be interesting to find out what goes on in their minds as they suck. . . .

RUTH:
Oh, I wish no woman would torment her senses. . . . I mean, no woman can truly fathom any man. Men are impossible to know. . . .

DAISY:
And maybe we women are bigger mysteries. So where do we begin?

RUTH:
Maybe from men's pillows!

DAISY: *(Laughing.)*
Hmm . . . that's cute. Why do you say that?

RUTH:
Because I think that's the gateway to anyone's soul or mind. . . .

DAISY:

    Interesting. . . .

RUTH:

    Can you imagine what goes on in people's minds as they lie there? *(Pause.)*

DAISY:

    Yes! We think we have and we know the men even as they lie beside us. But the true confidante is really the pillow. Can you imagine how many secrets we tuck in pillows . . . bank on pillows . . . impose on pillows? And I tell you, it doesn't matter whether we're male or female. It's mutual. Pillows are the real heroes. . . .

RUTH:

    NO, SHEROES!

DAISY:

    You're right; sheroes. Pillows are the true sheroes of love *(Pause.).* Think of how many tears and reservoirs of thoughts crossing our minds are invested in pillows!

RUTH:

    There's so much work out there for psychoanalysts. Perhaps my next subject of inquiry should be on the soul power of pillows . . . or simply, pillow power!

DAISY: *(Laughing.)*

    And bed power too!

RUTH:

    No, we'll leave the bed out of it. That will be too obvious. Leave that to women who won't live a normal life unless they're married to some man. . . .

DAISY:

    Who on his part is searching for other teaties to replace his mother's. Truly, now you've opened my eyes, I'm beginning to see these things in another light. Men are babies. Okei might have married me just to fulfil a need . . . to fill a vacancy, rather. You know what I mean?

RUTH:

    Oh, Daisy, don't be silly! Okei can't be as stupid as that.

DAISY:

    Why not? We just analyzed it. Every man is like Okei. In fact that is what his name means: man! They're in perpetual search of that mother-figure. That is why they can change their women just like that until they get one that's closest to fulfilling that lost-mother syndrome.

RUTH: *(Laughing.)*

    Oh, Daisy! You're crazy!

DAISY:
> True, they're all like that. Even the best of them. But who cares? Let him marry ten women until he finds one who can take the place of his mother. I tell you, I know my husband. I know who I'm dealing with. That woman is doomed, because she's only there as a figurehead. Men still use their mothers as measures for other women.

RUTH:
> I wonder why men have such a fixation on their mothers. Freud tried to explain it all, but I too have a problem with Freud—which is no subject for this discussion. *(Pause.)* You women who claim you're married deceive yourselves. In truth, husbands are married to their mothers . . . in their heads . . . in their minds, and they're more faithful to their mothers than to any other lover. I could swear to that. All they do is just use wives to cover up.

DAISY:
> You dare not make such statements in Idu.

RUTH:
> Why not?

DAISY:
> They'll say it's an abomination.

RUTH:
> Well, that's the basis of taboo . . . unnecessary silence. But the fact that they make it a taboo doesn't make it less of an improbable fact—or even a reality. Michel Foucault made some wonderful statements on that in *The Archeology of Knowledge*.

DAISY:
> Hmm . . .

RUTH:
> You remember Foucault? Or don't you anymore?

DAISY:
> Not really. . . .

RUTH:
> Well, that's what going into government or administration does to you: stuffs your brain with paper and power and money while disempowering all others . . . I mean senses.

DAISY:
> To some extent you are right. You win some; you lose some.

RUTH:
> Yes. But I know you married women are always losers.

DAISY:
> Maybe not always. . . . Women never really own their husbands until husbands lose their mothers.

RUTH:
> Oh, stop it, Daisy! You must hate his mother very much!

DAISY:
> Maybe not. But I tell you, men got a problem with their mothers. But mothers-in-law are pests. Pests! They must ensure that their sons are dried of emotion for other women; that guarantees them control. But at the same time, mothers-in-law pretend that they want their sons to grow up and mature, to nurture their own families. But they never cease to treat their sons as babies. Oh, Ruth! I've never known any naughtier babies than husbands. They just think they must continue sucking after being weaned from their mothers. When you are a wife, you're a servant, and all for no pay! You serve as his mother, one full-time job! You serve as his children's mother, another full-time job! You serve as his wife-roommate-caretaker—yet another full-time job! You serve as his cook, cleaner, steward, waiter, and janitor to clean up his mess! Oh, whoever invented the idea of marriage must be the greatest capitalist/extortionist ever born! Ugh!

RUTH:
> And this man must think I must be superhuman to be doing all these things! Wives must be superhuman!! *(They laugh.)*

DAISY:
> On the contrary, wives are treated as subhuman. . . . Wives are nothing but objects of marginality!

RUTH:
> You're putting it rather mildly. Wives are nothing but some glorified slaves who need to be liberated from "themselves."

DAISY:
> Sure! And for themselves! I have made my choice and am gonna have it "ma-way"!! *(She moves seductively toward RUTH. RUTH holds her tenderly.)* Discovering you is discovering myself . . . the lost self in me.

RUTH: *(Holding her closely.)*
> Oh, Daisy. Thank you.

DAISY:
> Our relationship is the best thing that ever happened to me in my life.

RUTH:
> You are so generous, dear.

DAISY:
> I'll be eternally grateful to you for opening up my vision to what my

horizons could be but which marriage and family had beclouded. I can see far now and clearly too. I feel born again.

RUTH: (*Laughing. A car pulls up at the gate but they are laughing so loud they do not hear it.*)
Yes, you are a born-again woman!

DAISY:
Until woman is born again in herself, she will not enter the "queen-dom" of life.

RUTH:
To find her heaven.

DAISY:
In her hen-dom! Until then she'll be forever sentenced to hellfire in the name of marriage.

RUTH:
Every woman needs to experience that rebirth in herself . . . in feminism. Every woman needs to discover herself.

DAISY:
In sisterhood. . . . (*Just then YEMOJA enters, carrying a heavy basket full of yams, tomatoes, and fruit on her head. YEMOJA is heavily weighed down by this burden. DAISY and RUTH study her wide-eyed and speechless. As YEMOJA attempts to lower the load from her head by herself, the basket topples over and the contents spill out. DAISY and RUTH jump aside instead of trying to help her. SHERIFAT is behind YEMOJA but DAISY and RUTH do not see her. When YEMOJA's burden falls, SHERIFAT, as far as her age and health permit, jumps forward to assist Yemoja as the load is falling. More than anything else, it is her scream for help that draws the attention of RUTH and DAISY to the newcomer: SHERIFAT, DAISY's mother-in-law. Silence. RUTH and DAISY exchange a knowing look. Everything has now spilled all over the floor. YEMOJA frantically begins to pick up the yams. SHERIFAT stands aside, bemused by the recent turbulence and the cold silence following it. DAISY's eyes search for whoever brought her mother-in-law to the house at this hour of the evening without informing her. The noise of a car trunk slamming closed is heard outside. DAISY's eyes follow the sound, and from the look on her face, it is obvious she knows her husband will walk in at any moment. SHERIFAT breaks the silence.*)

SHERIFAT:
Hmn . . . will no one welcome a woman into her house?

DAISY: (*Clumsily.*)
Well . . . ehm . . . you are welcome. I hope all is well. (*SHERIFAT begins to pace about the room.*)

SHERIFAT: *(Tersely.)*
All is well . . . as well as you left it. *(Pause.)* But I'm still waiting for someone to tell me whether this is my son's house I've walked into or whether I have entered the sheltered den of some lion. . . . *(She is saying this when OKEI enters.)*

OKEI: *(Walks in casually, goes over to kiss DAISY as he speaks.)*
Yeah, dear! How's everybody?

DAISY: *(Coldly.)*
"Everybody" is fine, I suppose. . . .

RUTH:
Welcome back. . . .

OKEI: *(As if just discovering her.)*
You're here too. . . . Hmm . . . how nice! *(OKEI is walking toward her now, his right hand thrust forward for a handshake. Surprisingly, RUTH tucks her hands into her jeans' pockets.)*

RUTH: *(Mildly sarcastic.)*
Superfine, thank you! And maybe not as insignificant as people seem to pretend we are.

OKEI:
Oh, come on, Ruth! You know I didn't mean to slight you. . . .

RUTH:
Well, so you say! But you men tend to have some programmed socially constructed signifiers for marginalizing . . .

OKEI:
Oh! There we go again! Signifiers and marginality! Please, please back off! I am just coming back from a long journey. And I tell you, my constitution right now is too weak for your feminist terrorism.

RUTH:
Ex-cuuuuse me!

DAISY:
Okei, wait a minute. What's all this about women and terrorism? Are you out of your mind? Ruth only made a statement.

OKEI: *(Tersely.)*
Fine! *(An uneasy silence reigns, except for intermittent noises from YEMOJA, who is still picking up the fallen pieces of yams from the floor. SHERIFAT pitifully studies YEMOJA as she works. SHERIFAT goes over to her, picks up some of the broken yams, and puts them in the basket.)*

SHERIFAT:
Is there nobody else in this house to help gather . . . *(Before she can finish the statement, OKEI interrupts.)*

TELL IT TO WOMEN

OKEI:
Yes, Yemoja! That's enough for now. Go and rest. (Exit YEMOJA. SHERIFAT *walks toward one of the sofas to sit down.*)

SHERIFAT:
Hmm . . . as the red-neck lizard says: "If I fall from a great height and no one nods or claps for me, I will nod for myself." This is my son's house. I do not need any invitation to come to my own house and I will come and sit when I like. . . . This is my own house. . . .

DAISY: (*Arrogantly.*)
Well, we have yet to see where that is written in the title or deed for this house. But for now, no one has said nobody should not come to her son's house. But certainly nobody is free to take any other for granted all the same, son or no son! People cannot just be walking into my house unannounced and expect an embrace. And I think I deserve to be informed that . . . (OKEI *is now very uneasy. He fights hard to hold back whatever threatens to explode from his mouth by biting his lips.*)

SHERIFAT:
Ehn! So I am now a stranger in my own son's house? Eh? Tell me Daazi! Am I a stranger in my son's house? I must now write for permission to come to my own son's house? Is that so, Okei? Answer me! (OKEI *is silent.*) So this is now what you have become . . . you are a stranger in your own house, Okei? (*Silence.*) Or are you no longer my son? If I didn't give birth to you, and if I didn't know whose stock you came from, I would have sworn you were not the son of Umudioka. (OKEI *is trying as best he can to be calm and keep the situation under control.*)

OKEI:
Well, Mama. It's not as bad as that yet. (*Turning to* DAISY.) Perhaps it's my fault, really. But I was caught up in the situation.

SHERIFAT: (*More incensed.*)
What situation, Okei? So you must now make apologies for my coming to your house? Idu, come and see! Come and hear! The barn has room enough for maize and not for yam? Idu, come! Come and see what they have turned my son into! You must bend to a mere wife—a chaff of grain—for me to stay in your house! Abomination! Ehn? Okei, you allow them to crush your manhood? Eh, Okei? (*Silence.*) Obida forbids palm wine! (*She bounces off, calling.*) Yemoja! Let me have my things now. I must return to the village. NOW! I have my place. I know my place. And I will not allow a bunch of people who do not know who they are to use me as a rag. . . . Yemoja! (YEMOJA *enters the room panting.*)

YEMOJA:

Here, our mother! (*OKEI intervenes again, trying to hold back his mother!.)*

OKEI:

Don't, Mama. Please. . . . Ajie, mother! Ojogwu, mother! *(He kneels to beg his mother. His mother studies him with compassion and motions to him to stand up. Okei stands and then turns to YEMOJA. He moves his mother toward the sofa to sit her down. He opens the refrigerator and offers her a drink, which she rejects. SHERIFAT sits biting her lips, her legs trembling. YEMOJA too understands the unspoken word weighing her down. At last, OKEI finds strength, raises his mother again and hands her over to YEMOJA, who leads her into the lower room. Exit YEMOJA and SHERIFAT. OKEI turns to look at Ruth, expecting her to leave them as a couple alone in privacy, but RUTH holds her ground and stares back at him until OKEI breaks his silence.)* And you too . . . Dr. Ruth. You will please leave us now.

DAISY:

No! She's not leaving here without me. No! And as a matter of fact, we were just getting ready to go out when you came in.

OKEI:

What?

DAISY:

Yes. I did not speak with water in my mouth, did I? I say Ruth is not leaving here without me. *(Silence.)*

OKEI:

I see.

DAISY:

I hope you do. . . . *(Silence.)*

OKEI:

So what's this all-important business that cannot wait till morning?

DAISY:

It's our business. Ruth and I have an engagement.

OKEI:

When?

DAISY:

Tonight. *(OKEI looks at his watch.)*

OKEI:

It's already midnight. Daisy, what engagement could be so important that you will be going out this late in the evening?

DAISY:

I'm no child. I can take care of myself. I'm not gonna take no instructions from no one. I ain't gonna do it! (*Silence.*) And don't ever ask me where and when I go. (*Emphatically.*) I don't need nobody to check on me. Don't worry about me.

OKEI: (*Trying to control his anger.*)

Easy . . . Daisy. And mind your language now. You can see I'm trying hard enough. But you are taking advantage of my willing silence. Over the past couple of weeks, I've observed that your language is progressively becoming foul, offensive . . . indecent. . . . You make me wonder if foulness is also a syndrome of liberation.

DAISY:

Your problem, not mine. A woman too reserves the right to choose her own words. Or don't you think so?

OKEI:

Oh come off it, Daisy! This has nothing to do with being a man or a woman. I see you are getting really obsessed about this thing. . . .

RUTH:

What an insult! Hey, man, I don't think you men smell less foul than women. So we're all caught up in the game of equality. Daisy, I've had more than my fair dose of insult piled upon injury for one day. See you, Daisy.

DAISY:

Ruth, please!

OKEI:

Leave her! Let her go!

RUTH:

Who are you to tell me to go? (*Silence.*) And come to think of it, I'm not leaving. (*She sits and begins to puff away at a cigarette. OKEI is visibly disturbed by the silence.*)

OKEI:

Okay, ladies. Right! Right there! Take your power, your mystic over man! Take it and go! I'm tired! And tired! Can't you pity a man who has come on a long journey to meet you from home? I am tired. Take whatever you will. You are subjecting me to a slow death. That's what you reduce men to in order to empower yourselves. No argument. One can only sound a note of warning: women, you now got the power, but power too intoxicates . . . it burns . . . it can burn you alive. But leave a man alone to mourn his own death. Go on your path of murdering, since you reject mothering. You women now use power to ruin the family. Do as you please, but let a man rest. Let a man lie down. You go on, fly. Fly! Fly high on our backs. But ride us well.

DAISY:

You are just pretending, Okei. You are not tired. You are afraid of women. You are not tired, man. You are afraid. Tiredness is a mask you invent to hide your fear. Go on man, confess. You're afraid of us.

OKEI: (*Sardonic laughter.*)

Afraid of what? Ugh! Are you joking, woman? That's the biggest joke of the century! That should go into the Guinness Book of Records. (*Seriously choosing his words.*) Women are a Huge Joke! Ha! Ha! Ha! Women?

DAISY AND RUTH: (*Together.*)

And what are men? Larger jokes! Eternal jokers!!

OKEI:

As you say. But leave the fools alone. You fly with your wisdom and never perch!

RUTH: (*Leaving.*)

Daisy, see you soon. I'm leaving, and mark you, Mr. Okei, it is not because you say so or wish it. I'm leaving because I got business to do.

OKEI:

That suits me just fine. We break even.

DAISY:

And I'm coming with you (*DAISY moves toward RUTH as she's opening the door.*)

OKEI:

Why can't you be reasonable? What decent woman goes out at this time of night? And a married woman for that matter?

DAISY:

When you go away on your own "business" and come back and tell me you have been attending your "professional meetings," no one asks you for any reasons or explanations. Do they? So leave me alone! Ruth and I have a project together. . . . The launching of the program of Better Life for Rural Women comes up soon, and both of us are coordinators. Take note, mister man. We too, like you, have our (*emphatically*) PROFESSIONAL CAREERS. That too must be given priority. I too have a career. Understand?

OKEI: (*Cynically.*)

Yeah! Go on! Careeeer wo-man! Go on! And lose your sense of propriety along with your craze for career. But other people with common sense would have waited to settle their husband and mother-in-law before going on a rampage with their new "isms." . . . Ugh!

TELL IT TO WOMEN

Fe-mi-ni-sm! That is the newest meal for malnourished Africans. Yeah! Dish it out! Let's get bloated on it! If you won't know yourselves, maybe you should let others tell you women what you really are. Someone should tell you that people are getting tired of your feminist garbage. Anyone who pretends to have intelligence should have the common sense not to dish out dogmas in such large doses so people don't bloat or choke. But you so-called educated women either mistake book sense for wisdom or dismiss the common for the ordinary and inferior.

DAISY:
Whatever you mean by that! By the way, how common is common sense, mister? If yours is, mine isn't.

OKEI: *(Ignoring her.)*
Fly to any height you want to and make sure you perch high enough, woman! And no one need tell you about downfalls, since you know too much. Burn all bridges on your road to freedom! But make sure you'll never take those routes again. And when you are done with your rampage, I will still insist that anyone with sense would have chosen some other time to go pushing their careers into the night rather than when their husband returns home from a long trip and when their mother-in-law, who incidentally is a woman too like them, comes to visit. And better still, when that mother-in-law, who's being marginalized (to use your own terminology), is a key factor in a project they're obsessed with, shows up unexpectedly. Go on and rave and fight and conquer everyone until you have no other enemy to fight but yourself! Just go on. Your victims are waiting. Your victims have assembled and are awaiting your manslaughter. So what are you waiting for? Equality? That you won long ago, woman! Now you do not fight for equality but for the extermination of every "other," including your fellow women!!! No, woman! You do not fight for equality, but for conquest and extermination of every other on your path to destruction!!! *(Pause.)* People with better intelligence would have found out first what business brings a frog running in the daytime instead of . . .

DAISY: *(Rather subdued.)*
So it's because of the program that Mama is here? *(Silence. DAISY and RUTH exchange glances. DAISY bends down to touch OKEI's cheek.)* Won't you tell me? *(Silence.)* Won't you speak? *(Silence.)* Okay. Let's forget what happened tonight. But you must remember, you started it all. . . . You caused the aggravation. *(DAISY again bends down to stroke OKEI's cheek and looks him straight in the eye. RUTH senses that DAISY's tone is changing and becoming conciliatory. She cannot hide her jealousy.)*

RUTH:
> Well, Mr. and Mrs. Okei, I must be leaving now.

DAISY: *(Awkwardly.)*
> Oh, you are?

RUTH:
> Yes, mam. . . .

OKEI:
> I wish you well, lady. I'm certain that there won't be anyone left in your queendom after your coronation. Man will always be your ultimate price for freedom and ascension to the throne of power.

DAISY: *(Quickly.)*
> Eh, Okei. Don't say that again. The matter is settled now. Ruth and Mama and I, we'll sort things out. (*RUTH is now well at the door.*) Okay, Ruth! I will keep you informed about developments. See you tomorrow.

RUTH: *(Coldly.)*
> Until then. (*RUTH leaves. OKEI begins to unbutton his shirt and relaxes on the sofa.*)

DAISY: *(Coaxing OKEI now.)*
> You know I am not usually like this.

OKEI:
> How?

DAISY:
> Well you know . . . I'm not the termagant you present me to be. . . . You caused the aggravation.

OKEI: *(Arrogantly.)*
> We heard that already. Any other news?

DAISY:
> Hmm . . . well . . . you are to blame for all these . . . I mean your attitude. . . .

OKEI:
> Of course! Who else? Who else is to blame but me? I accept. Every fault must be mine. I accept the role of sacrificial lamb on the high altar of your ascension, woman. Whose blood could make for better atonement but mine? Always . . . always. It's okay. Time shall be the ultimate judge.

DAISY: *(Ignoring him.)*
> So Mama is here because of our launching?

OKEI: *(Still lost in thought.)*
> Handsome species woman is. Wonderful! Wildly exotic and in-

flammable too. Except one never really knows which part of her will ignite first. . . .

DAISY:
Well, be careful now. I'm doing everything possible to resolve this matter. But don't take advantage of me now. Don't insult us. I don't have any stomach for insults! (OKEI's *silence becomes progressively irritating to* DAISY.) You're taking advantage of my moment of yielding. (*Walking away from him now.*) You men are just nothing but suckers!

OKEI: (*In absolute disgust.*)
And you women are nothing but fakers . . . mother-fakers! You are nothing but some exotic waste dumped on the human species. (OKEI *stops. Silence.*)

DAISY:
Hey, man! Why did you stop? Go on! It's getting more entertaining. (OKEI *is silent.*) Hmm . . . maybe while you men wait for your certificate as teachers of women, we might fuel you up by giving you a thunderous round of applause. (*She claps for* OKEI.) Hey, hurray! Hurray for men! (OKEI *is untying his shoelaces now and completely ignores* DAISY.) Hey, what's up? You beaten? You feel you've been played out of your own game? We can't always be winners, can we? (OKEI *rises, goes over to the refrigerator, fetches himself a drink, pours it out and starts to drink. Silence except for his very loud belching.* DAISY *moves her face away to avoid the bad breath. She's still embarrassed and trying to be playful.*) Instead of wasting this precious time on nothing, why don't you tell me what's happening with the program for rural women and what brought Mama here? I hope you do that for me, teacher. (OKEI *takes a sip.*) I'm still waiting for his lordship to tell me why Mama is here. (*Pause.*) I hope that isn't too much of a favor to ask his majesty. (*Silence.*) Hey, man, tell me what you are doing with your Mama in the city!

OKEI:
Precisely. That is where you should have started instead of terrorizing everybody. But to prove your rare kind of expertise, you must first go off on a tangent. Mama is here for the launching. The Umuada sent her on their behalf to assist Yemoja. The rural women will be here any time now.

DAISY: (*Rapidly and nervously.*)
But why? We haven't sent for them yet! We are not yet ready for them! Oh, God! Let these women not be my death! (OKEI *is guzzling his drink now with a smile playing on his lips.*) The minister has only just fixed the date for the launching. And we are not prepared yet.

Why do these women want to overtake us? And if they come now, no arrangement has been made for their accommodation. Okei, you know them better. I'm lost now and confused. How am I to deal with these village women?

OKEI:

Wait a minute. What is my business in all this? I thought I was the enemy. I'm only the bearer of the news and, as our people say, a message cannot kill its bearer. Why must you rope me in? You're being utterly unfair, woman! How can you make a man chief celebrant at his own funeral?

DAISY: *(Drifting.)*

So the women are coming? *(Sighs.)* My god! These women will be my ruin. . . . I must see Mama! *(She rises.)* Where is she? Will these women be my ruin?

OKEI:

I haven't said that either. All I know is that the wind is blowing strong toward the city. Storms are ravaging the very root of the family to the extent that sometimes one can't tell which storm is more destructive: wind or woman.

DAISY: *(Ignoring him and lost in thought.)*

And so the women are coming? My god! *(Turning to OKEI, who is gleefully humming a tune to himself.)* Why are the women in such a hurry anyway?

OKEI:

Are you asking me? Am I a woman now? Ask your disciples! After all, you are their leader . . . and you started it all. *(Pause.)* You set the bush on fire and now turn around to me, your victim, to quench the fire. Lord have mercy! You women are something else! Lord have mercy! Never forsake me in these times of trouble . . . troublesome women! Lord save me from these . . . oh, what is a man to call them? *(Pause. OKEI stares at the door and suddenly bursts into laughter.)* God save us! Who will tell God? Who will tell him that the man he created is at the brink of extinction by his fellow creation? *(DAISY, realizing that OKEI is now beginning to gain the upper hand on her psychologically, tries to toughen herself.)*

DAISY:

That is your own God. The God I know is WOMAN!! *(OKEI laughs sardonically.)*

OKEI:

Armageddon! Woman! You've dethroned God too? *(Pause.)* That is interesting . . . interesting that God too has now been stripped of his powers and is now woman. Hurray to woman! Hurray to feminists! (*He spits.*) Baaaah! Woman! Incredible! (*Pause.*) So God is now woman? (*Brief silence.*) No! God cannot be woman. They say with God, everything is possible. But I know one thing for sure. God cannot be woman. Otherwise how is man to survive? How's the world to survive if God is woman? If woman is God . . . if God is woman, how are we to have rain? No, woman! You are not God! God died in your womb when you invented another image for yourself and threw away his own! (*DAISY is more concerned with the imminent problem than with OKEI's diatribe on women.*)

DAISY:
God, what are you doing to me?

OKEI:
What you are doing to others! God is clever, and since you seek to destroy others, he too will use your own instruments against you. The women are coming to be the hand of God. . . .

DAISY:
The God I know is just. I will not be harmed. . . .

OKEI: (*Laughing.*)
Do you know the story of Obida, sister of Onokwu/Yemoja and Goddess of Wealth in Ogwashi-uku? She only dishes out her wealth to deserving sons and daughters. Not just anybody. And you cannot bribe or command her. Obida is the mother who's obsessed with justice. What is Obida's cognomen? She's called the supreme mother, Goddess of Justice, whose breasts are so large that they droop like coconuts to her knees. Obida too is the great mother who feeds the world with her eternally flowing milk, But then too, Obida is the Goddess of Justice, who is so stern toward her erring children that she crushes the testicles of her erring sons. Do you know Obida or Onokwu/Yemoja? I know you do not. That is why I must tell you. These were the women, these were the mothers, not the chaffs floating along now and wearing the faces of women. (*Silence.*) I know this as a rule of thumb. . . . "Don't start a war you cannot finish." It's one thing to start a revolution; it's another thing to be able to control it. Management too is an art, you know. Go tell it to women! (*OKEI goes wild having his fun at DAISY's expense. But DAISY is determined not to be provoked into any further argument.*)

DAISY:
Enough, Okei! Thanks for the entertainment. Thanks too for the homily. But enough! I've heard more than enough homilies in my lifetime. So enough of it now! I'm fed up. All I'm saying is that this is bad timing. The women have chosen the worst time for coming

to the city because it is clear nobody is ready for them yet, not even me.

OKEI:

My apologies then. But I'm only a passenger on this ship, and you are supposed to be the captain. Just insure that you pilot us well or the ship will capsize, and we'll all go adrift and perish.

DAISY: *(Vexed.)*

Don't you think this is bad timing for your mocking?

OKEI:

Well, my apologies, Your Excellency! Pardon! Pardon, madam! But . . .

DAISY:

But what?

OKEI:

Don't underestimate the power of women . . . I mean real . . . rural women. Don't underestimate what you do not comprehend. And don't even try to oversimplify it. These rural women may look shallow to you. Remember as you're stepping onto unsure ground that still waters can run deep.

DAISY:

Granted. But I still insist they are taking the matter too seriously or they're simply being childish. You know, like kiddies who've found some new toys? These women too got to learn to wait. They got to learn too that waiting is part of the game.

OKEI:

You see? Note your words. For you the whole mission is a game . . . of power. For them it is life! It is a matter of their own survival in a world that is disappearing. A world whose control is being taken out of their hands. For you the issue is power and equality. For them it is life. It is their life! Are you then telling me that you are playing a game with people's lives? *(Pause.)* That is criminal!

DAISY:

Oh, stop, Okei! Stop! Stop making it sound so tragic . . . so philosophical, and as if we're shifting the women out of power. They never had it anyway. Nobody has denied them life or any such thing. So just stop all that propaganda. The point I'm making is that if the women are coming already, they will be coming too soon. This place is not ready for them yet.

OKEI:

Then somebody must be flashing the wrong signal somewhere. Either that, or you people are simply enmeshed in your own rhetoric.

You people must be using them for a huge joke, and that's criminal. You're playing with other people's lives and their place in it. You must appreciate the difference between you and traditional women. While you double-talk and make simple things sound complex, they're too straightforward . . . too simple.

DAISY:
Precisely! That is the first truth you have spoken. Rural folks are too simplistic!

OKEI:
No! Don't distort statements. Rural folks are not simplistic. They may be simple, even simple-minded, but that does not mean they are simplistic. They're completely different things: simplicity and simplistic!

DAISY:
I hear you, defender of the faithful. I hear you. I wish you could run fast and tell your disciples that they are putting others under undue pressure. The blueprint for the program is still in process. There is no concrete plan yet for the Better Life Program. All we are doing now is simply theorizing the condition of women and proposing new grounds for their empowerment.

OKEI:
Yeah! Theory . . . theory . . . the new academic epidemic. Theory! Go on and theorize, Your Holiness, our professors of nothing! Our ultra-modern puritans, inventors of new cultism(s) and alchemy in the name of academy. Go on with your gimmicks. But note, the world is fed up with your terrorizing theories. . . . (DAISY *stands aside, watching* OKEI, *not with anger but with obvious interest and amusement as he raps away his disgust on women and academics.*) Your new crown of theory will soon be capped with a new "tion" or "ism" so it can attract attention in your cults and circles of eggheads who float in the air hallucinating and speaking in tongues in the name of intellectualism. That is what you feminists, especially, have reduced the academy to: cultism. Our institutions are no longer citadels of learning, but factories of hot-burning ultra-violent words: showrooms and parade grounds for new jargons and jaw-breaking words to bamboozle willing minds. You're daily competing for and spinning out new jargons and jaw-breaking words like overdressed, expensive-looking dolls are no more than toys for mammies and baby-less mothers. So you swing from structuralism to poststructuralism to Marxism to feminism to postfeminism to deconstruction to postdeconstruction and genderism and lesbianism and the new ethnicity and all in the name of oppositionality and epistemologies

of closets of nothings. Signifying this; spacifying that! What are they specifying? NOTHING!!! And for nothing they get stuffed with fat paychecks and . . . theories and treacheries . . . and . . . ! (*As OKEI is spilling out all this, DAISY is overwhelmed and intrigued by her husband's new hysteria; she goes over to the refrigerator to fetch him a drink. OKEI is completely oblivious of DAISY now.*) And . . . and when these academics are women? Ugh! God save us from internal, eternal damnation! (*He takes a deep breath.*) Modern academics no longer construct knowledge. They fabricate magic words to mystify others. They pull new wool over the eyes of those they think are blind, hoping to camouflage their shallowness in the name of specialization, expertism, dogmatism, and . . . and . . . (*DAISY, with an ironic smile, offers OKEI a drink. OKEI, startled by his own voice, which is now heightened by the silence around him, stops, turns around to find DAISY, now with a glass of water in her hand.*)

DAISY: (*Smiling.*)

Are you okay? (*Offering him the glass of water.*) Well, take this. I thought you might need it. (*OKEI stares at her without accepting the offer.*) I didn't know you were that far gone in paranoia. Interesting how and when we discover people around us. (*OKEI is silent.*) It's not women you fear. But rather enlightened women. I'll take note of that. . . . (*She goes over to him, trying to make him sit on the sofa. OKEI is backing away from DAISY.*) Relax and sit here. The rural women are on their way. I'll go down to speak with Mama. . . . (*Calling.*) Mama! Mama!

OKEI:

You think she will come to you just like that? How do you hope to lead her when you don't even know her? You exist in two separate worlds. Her world is completely alien to yours. And if you continue with this arrogance and condescension, I tell you, you're going to be surprised, for I know the rural world. It is a world where tradition is held sacred and people truly care about their pride, their family name and uncompromising sense of identity. And how do they achieve that? Through communal reinforcement of issues of identity and solidarity! Hey, my learned one, if you want to win the rural women over, you must come down from your ivory tower and dialogue with them on equal terms, and with respect too. Not this talking-down attitude by which you intimidate them from your high altars of academe, from which you flash neon lights to dazzle them. You must be humble to learn from them. True knowledge humbles. But for reckless people like you, knowledge empowers to the point of intoxication. You got to change your attitude to appreciate and win the rural women over.

TELL IT TO WOMEN

Daisy: *(Flirting.)*

Oh, come on, Okei. Don't get so emotional about these people. You miss the point.

Okei:

What point?

Daisy:

Well, you talk about us winning the rural women over as if we were waging war against them.

Okei:

So against who are you waging the war then? Against men?

Daisy:

Well, whoever . . . whatever . . . the enemy . . . I mean . . .

Okei:

Daisy, no need to start stammering now. You've gone too far to be stammering. Have you thought carefully about your own world, our world, before you jumped onto this feminist bandwagon? You can't just transfer ideologies from one cultural milieu to another. You better think seriously before you get grounded. You feminists may need to reconsider your politics of confrontation and oppositionality; your Cartesian ideology of this or that. Your binary logic of EITHER/OR cannot stand in a world like Idu, where everything is seen in terms of dualisms: where everything is related and complementary: man AND woman, good AND evil; night AND day, etc., etc. Where you envision opposites, they envision difference and complementarity. That is fundamental if you want to enter and capture the mind of Idu. There is no other way. You elite women think that knowledge is the exclusive preserve of the Western mind. Just wait until you enter the labyrinth of the African traditional ethos. And until you descend from your great heights, you feminist ideologues, you will remain strangers, not only to your world, but to their world. My learned woman, you must understand. These rural women may adore you from a distance, but they won't let you take them for a ride. But who am I to challenge the National Director of Women's Affairs? It's your space, ride on! It's your war, real or imagined. It's your war. And I'm only an observer. Ride on, but ride with caution. That is my only advice to you.

Daisy:

I hear you. *(Pause.)* Maybe you're right. *(She raises her left arm, reads her watch and rises immediately.)* How time passes! I must go to Mama now! *(Hurriedly, she opens the door leading to the lower room. She stands there silently for a short while, perhaps gathering her thoughts for the encounter. She steals a look at Okei as he pulls off his* shoes and gathers them in his hands in readiness to enter his bedroom for sleep. She takes a deep breath and begins her slow descent into the lower room, where her mother-in-law has been accommodated. Slow fade-out.)

MOVEMENT THREE
Earth Meets Sea

(*The time is near dawn.* SHERIFAT *and* YEMOJA *together perform the traditional ritual honoring the Earth Goddess and Onokwu/Yemoja, Goddess of the Sea, for whom the women are devotees and priestesses. Because they are in the city, away from the village where the traditional ritual items are readily available, they improvise with water and garden eggs in place of palm wine and Kolanut.* YEMOJA *drums while* SHERIFAT *recites the incantation to which* YEMOJA *responds.*)

SHERIFAT: (*Pouring libation onto the earth.*)
Ani, Earth Goddess. Source of our comings! Source of our goings! Ani, eat. Womb that never fills! (YEMOJA *drums,* SHERIFAT *pours more libation.*) Ani, eat! Ani, stomach that forever bears all and swallows all. (*Drums.*) Ani, Earth Goddess, mother whose belly swallows and shelters and keeps all! (*Drums.*) Ani! Lips sealed always, only letting out her secrets when she wills. Ani! Lead us! Hold us that we may not fall in the stormy weather! (*Drums. Drums. Drums.*) Twin sister of Onokwu/Yemoja! Hand that molds. Steady our feet that the new storm may not tear us apart for this world to see our nakedness! Onokwu/Yemoja, Goddess of the Sea! Mouth with neither beginning nor end! Lead us that we may not walk when the earth yawns. (YEMOJA *drums. Enter* DAISY. *Silence overtakes the drums and the invocation of the goddesses.* SHERIFAT *and* YEMOJA *stare at* DAISY. DAISY *breaks the silence and looks* YEMOJA *straight in the eye.*)

DAISY:
Go on, drum! Drum, Voodoo Princess! (YEMOJA *fidgets but is not as nervous as she used to be. Silence returns until* SHERIFAT *speaks.*)

SHERIFAT:
These drums obey only voices of goddesses, not the ranting of some foul seasonal winds. Their rhythms too strange to many, hard of hearing. Only devotees of nature hear and join their chorus and their laughter. . . .

DAISY: (*Pointing at* YEMOJA.)
Like that one too?

SHERIFAT: (*Charged.*)
Yes! Like her, mouth of the Earth. Yes, like Yemoja, the silent one,

whose heart is deep enough to drink the world. Yes, like her—Yemoja!! Has anyone ever told you that this woman, this Yemoja here before you, is a divine priestess and devotee of the goddess whose image she bears? How dare you! How dare you rub her face with mud? We are visions of goddesses. You call us women! How dare you? Beware! Beware, you who pride yourselves on draining the unknown contents of the sea! Beware of drowning in the sea! And don't forget: Yemoja, the woman of Idu, is the divine soul of the Goddess of the Sea and Earth. How dare you put a wedge between land and sea? Note, Onokwu/Yemoja is the womb of Earth. How can you empty the Earth's content? Yemoja is a woman just like you! Yemoja is a mother just like you! Yemoja is a wife just like you. You cannot push her around and throw her about like a fading rag. Yemoja too belongs to the world and knows her place in it. How dare you take away her dignity of womanhood? (*Pause.*) And note ... that unlike you, mere woman, Yemoja is the prime woman and mother whose soul is deeply rooted in the soil ... deeply rooted in the land unlike you, creature of many undefined faces, who are neither here nor there. What else could be more death for you women on the edge of the world? What death could be worse?

(SHERIFAT *turns her back on* DAISY. YEMOJA *is uneasy. Silence.*)

DAISY: (*She is irritated but trying to control her anger.*)
Haven't you said enough yet? I am trying ... hard ... but don't. Don't push me to the limit. ... Please ... please, don't push me too far or we will all be sorry. (*Pause.*) I see you have not yet forgotten the events of last night. (*Silence.*) But ... but yesterday should be behind us now. (*Pause.*) I came for something else. ...

SHERIFAT:
At the mouth of the sea?

DAISY:
At the heart of woman!

SHERIFAT:
To silence the drums?

DAISY:
To ask why you have come so early ahead of the women?

SHERIFAT:
I see ... I see. ... That is what you want to know. I have not come to eat your food in the city. I have come to tighten the strings of the drum whose tongue has been split. Our drums are hoarse and slit from your battering. That is what I have come to do. You, woman without tribe or tongue! Woman, take away your nails from the

drums; they bleed and cry for help! And I . . . we have come to dry the tears of the wailing drums. So, my new woman, take away your painted nails. Our drums need no other colors; they have a soul of their own. Take your painted nails away! I've come to dry the face of drums drenched with tears by your nails. What else am I to tell you, my new woman of masks and colors?

DAISY:
I hear you. I . . . we . . . can mend it together. . . .

SHERIFAT:
Ha! Ha! Ha! You make me laugh. How can you mend it when you're not trained in the art of being woman? You know it's not just enough for one to bear the image of woman. You must know what it is to be woman, and accept, with dignity, what it means to be woman. You must know woman and know her and her place in the circle to acquire her healing hand. How can you speak woman's mind when you defile woman and do not know her, my woman of strange faces?

DAISY: *(She chooses her words carefully.)*
If that is what you've come for, I have no problem with your mission. Except that your mission needs to be clarified. (DAISY *turns to* YEMOJA *and eyes her.*) Yemoja, go upstairs and cook the meal! You are taking advantage of her presence to leave your chores undone. If you hang around her like some apron string, who's to prepare breakfast for this household? Yemoja, answer me!

SHERIFAT:
You, Daisy, you!

DAISY:
Don't push me too far now! I was talking to Yemoja, not to you. Yemoja is paid to do a job. It's a bargain.

SHERIFAT:
A bargain, yes! She sold herself to you to be used as a rag to clean your anus. *(Brief silence.)*

DAISY:
Mama, why don't you come off this? My business in this house is with Yemoja. Why do you come between us? I've tried hard to accommodate you . . . I mean to tolerate you as my mother-in-law . . . but . . . but . . . since you came here, everything seems to have changed. And I want to have control over . . .

YEMOJA:
What Mama is saying . . .

DAISY:
Just stop right there! Who has made you our spokeswoman?

SHERIFAT:

> That is what I should be asking you! Who made you the town crier for women? (*Uneasy silence.*) Well, if I must tell you, Yemoja's business is my business.

DAISY:

> I see. . . .

SHERIFAT:

> You see nothing.

DAISY:

> Then we shall see. Yemoja, go upstairs immediately.

SHERIFAT:

> Yemoja, I say stay!!! (*Tense silence.* YEMOJA *is torn in two.*)

YEMOJA: (*Slowly but firmly.*)

> Sherifat, our mother. She is your daughter-in-law. You are her mother-in-law. I am only an outsider in your midst. If it is her wish . . . that I go, I will. . . .

SHERIFAT: (*With fire in her eyes.*)

> You are going nowhere, Yemoja! Do you hear me? You are not going anywhere out of your place! Not while I am here with you!! So now pick up the drum. Drum! Drum! Drum, Yemoja! Who is afraid of the drums?

YEMOJA:

> Well, if you say so, our mother! Where I come from, age speaks. Age commands respect. If our mother commands me to stay, who then can be against me? (YEMOJA, *strengthened, picks up her drum.* DAISY *leaves in anger.* YEMOJA *and* SHERIFAT *burst into laughter.*)

SHERIFAT:

> You see? She left! I have told you that night and day never meet!! How can you fear to speak when you have the drums? How can you fear, you who know when night opens its eyelids? Why must you fear? You, who know the sun's course through your finger tips?

YEMOJA:

> I have reason to fear, mother Sherifat. But the hen too sweats . . . she sweats. Lost in the night in the city with the moon covered with roofs that shoot high up into the sky and light bulbs cover the eyes of stars, the hen sweats, mother Sherifat. How can I not fear this new world? I know myself. I am Yemoja, the spirit of Yemoja. Idu knows me. But here in this city, I have no name. Nobody knows me . . . or rather, all they call me is "she." Why, our mother, will you expect god herself not to be afraid when the tides are so high and waves blow us away from home into foreign shores? Mother! Our

drums are intimidated into silence in this strange land that mocks Earth herself. Its loud laughter far into the night shatters the whiskers of Earth and dries the very essences of rivers and seas. In this condition, how can we not mourn their silences, our silences, mother Sherifat? Are these not the dying days of our land? *(Brief silence.)*

SHERIFAT:
And that is why you must be strong, my child. The women look up to you. You are their ears, here, in the city. You are the spirit of the women of the land. Their ears itch for sounds of new drums to wake them up, and move their feet forward. Why do you allow the offal, leftovers from the entrails of people with white disease, to muffle you into silence?

YEMOJA:
I understand what you mean. But times are no longer the same. And we would be fools not to know. These treacherous times leave us with lips that quiver. Our drums no longer rouse the spirits of our land. For this, I followed the new masquerade, dancing new steps to hear the language of the new drums we thought might give power to our own. We let our feet dance and follow new steps to hear the language of new drums to lengthen the tongue of our drums long slit by violent winds from the West. Our vision was to extend the tongue of our drums. But here . . . I am here . . . we are here, so far away from home, so distant from the throat of our talking drums! Where we go from here, I still cannot tell. All I see is us going. And though we do not see the end of the road, I know we must go beyond here.

SHERIFAT: *(Passionately.)*
And for this, daughters of Idu sing your blessings. You, Yemoja, are the salt of the Earth. If the Sea loses salt, what else is left for an embittered humanity? Eh, Yemoja? How can the Sea lose its salt so fast? How can people now wash their feet in your waters? The Sea's salt burns, you know! Are you not Yemoja? Burn, Yemoja, burn! Burn these spiteful feet defacing the face of mothers . . . our Earth . . . our land! Yemoja, the women await your flames on violent tongues that lick the Earth dry! Burn, Yemoja! The Earth awaits your call. The Sea awaits your call. Burn! Yemoja, the Sea burns!!! *(SHERIFAT has become so passionate that YEMOJA goes over and takes her hands tenderly, for she is quivering.)* And heals too!

SHERIFAT: *(The two women are locked in each other's arms.)*
I know!

YEMOJA:
I know . . . but . . .

SHERIFAT:
> But what?

YEMOJA: *(She steps aside.)*
> There in Idu my feet were planted on Earth. Here in this hell or cell called city, my feet wobble. I walk on air. I am myself no more. I am a stranger. I am a new hen in a new environment, one foot up, one foot down. Hawks circle in the skies. Where am I to run? I do not belong here. I know not their paths . . . which ones are safe. I want to run. I feel I'm running, but my feet are tied. I run in one spot. The enemy is so near, ready to pounce on me. I cry aloud but the city replies to me with its loud, deafening laughter. I pray for help . . . and I'm here waiting still. . . . I am the hen newly relocated. I want to walk, one foot up, one foot down, surveying the environment. And until I know where I stand, I cannot put my two feet down.

SHERIFAT:
> When will that time come, Yemoja? When? Is this your voice I hear, Yemoja? Or has some other voice taken you over? You sound distant and strange even to yourself. So how can the women who sent you here recognize you?

YEMOJA:
> I understand. I may be a disappointment to you, and to them all. But I tell you, mother, the day is not as bright as it was when the sun broke the face of the sky. So many hot waters have rushed so fast that the land now loses her face to the sky. How then can the lips go chattering when they are losing their teeth? Think of it. *(Pause.)* And you know this yourself. I came here with promises . . . promises to give better life to the women of Idu. But here I am, still confined more than ever before. Here I am, a total stranger, cleaning another's mess, shining another's shoes. Am I still Yemoja? I cannot be sure now. Daily, they push me into the corner and then turn around and stare at me as if I carry shit on my wrapper. Mother Sherifat! You call me Yemoja. The city cares not for my name. . . . It cares not to know my name. The city drowns all names with its hoarse laughter. And so to survive, I perch in the corner assigned to me, hoping that the hawk hovering for meat to scavenge never gets me. And once I'm sure of this little space they have pushed me into, I will show them Yemoja is here on their doorstep. The world will hear that Yemoja came to the city. They will hear. They will know the difference. But for now I stay while trying to name this corner . . . this space in this place. . . . All I know now is that in the corner, I'm at the bottom of the ladder, taking orders from everyone else.

(*Sighs.*) Oh, if only it were just taking orders from men and children! But taking orders from my fellow women? God!! What have you done to Yemoja? Taking orders from those I thought were my sisters? Those who led me into this cell with sweet words? Oh, how they spoke of strengths in sisterhood and oneness and equality of men and women! Strange how modern men and women are! Strange how many gaps exist between our world and the world of our new sisters! God, where is the way? Where now is the truth between missing words? (*YEMOJA bursts into tears. SHERIFAT draws near, pulls her to her bosom as if rocking her and begins intoning words of comfort, as if singing a lullaby.*)

SHERIFAT:
Let it out, child. Spill out the bitter content of your heart. And all will be well.

YEMOJA:
Mother, I'm still searching . . . searching for the place, for the word that was promised. Where is the word? Where has the word gone? God, I hear people talk and talk. God, I want to hear you speak now. Chukwu Abieme, the power whose words never fail, I want to hear the word, your word! Give me the strength to wait to find the word and tell it to women! God, the city knows no sister. The city knows no brother and father and mother! (*Pause.*) How close am I to this, my new-found sister? This is what cripples my movement, mother Sherifat. You too have seen for yourself. Since I came here, they've used and abused me. I've been a thing left in a corner of the house. I'm told I cannot enter the bedroom. I'm told I cannot eat with the family, as if I had the white disease. Yemoja, DON'T! DON'T! Don't do this! Don't do that! And even the spaces and places I owned in the village, I no longer have. The freedom I had to till the land and earn my living, the independence I had to feed me and my children, I no longer have. Why? Because here I must look into someone's face to be paid for only what pleases her as my new lord . . . Her Majesty, Daisy Okei, QUEEN OF A NAMELESS CITY! I have tested life in the city, mother Sherifat, and I wonder if my life in the village was not much better than the confusion the city has to offer me. Mother Sherifat, the city takes away the power of women. Can't you see the women roaming the streets with their wares?

SHERIFAT: (*Trying to brighten YEMOJA's mood.*)
Some are hawking their bodies too! (*YEMOJA smiles. Brief, reflective silence.*)

YEMOJA:
I have seen the city, mother Sherifat. The city glows and laughs with

borrowed teeth from strange lands. All we want, mother Sherifat, is our land. Let these city people bring their light and pipe-borne water to Idu, where the land is ours. Only then will the better life be for us and not for them. If women of Idu are to have the better life, these people should not take our life away and give us their own. They may claim they have a life in the city. I tell you, mother, they have no soul.

SHERIFAT: *(Smiling.)*

I hear you, my daughter. What we need to live is not their life, but our own. This is why, for us, the better life means where we have a hold, not where we remain strangers and objects to be ordered around at the will of others.

YEMOJA:

And what is now more tragic is that we have to be displaced even by our kind, the so-called sisters.

SHERIFAT:

Well, Yemoja. The ancestors are not dead . . . and the gods of Idu are not sleeping. The ancestors hear you. Our gods hear you. But you must be patient and steady your feet to move when the season turns. (SHERIFAT *resorts to chants and the drums.*) My daughter. Let me sing for you the song of life. It is the song of life. It is the song called PATIENCE. Patience is the song of life. Patience is the song for life. The other name of life is patience. The other name for life is patience. Child, let me sing . . . let me sing for you the song of life. . . . Let me sing to you about patience, the conqueror of pain, the one who survives when others die. It is of patience . . . patience . . . patience. Patience is the code for life. Patience is the word we are searching for. You cannot find it outside yourself. How can you find yourself outside yourself? Be patient, daughter of Okeke! Defender of Idu! Master wrestler of Umudioka! Knot the bleeding umbilicus with patience . . . patience . . . patience. . . . For patience is the lasting cord of life. Patience . . . patience . . . patience . . . patience . . . is the cord that binds the fragmented pieces of our hopes together. For now, pull your wrapper together. And tie it tight. (SHERIFAT *stops drumming.*) The women are on their way. And they look up to you, for you are the hope sent ahead to till the ground for the seasons to come. The launching of the Better Life will soon be here. And do not forget that Idu women sent you ahead of them to learn what needs to be done so they can stand. But you, Yemoja, must find the light to show them the way. You must not fail the women when the time comes.

YEMOJA:

I agree with you, mother. But even a lamb being led to slaughter smells blood along the path and bleats in fear, sensing its own end. Mother Sherifat, you know where I am coming from. I have already lost everything . . . everybody; my husband, my children, my father, mother! All in search of myself in this mist, where only money gives sight, where only money can give you place and position. I have seen it all, mother Sherifat! The new world is a wilderness. The new world is unlike the village where you belong, no matter what. Mother Sherifat, I never knew that anyone could be homeless until I stumbled on this wilderness. Don't you see the homeless? In spite of their saying we're poor, did you ever see anyone homeless in the village? But here they are with the Better Life where people are homeless. Here I see the Better Life is no life at all!! No matter how poor, everyone in Idu has a home . . . has a place. But here in the modern world? Ugh! Mother have you seen people living under the bridges?

SHERIFAT:
Of course I have!

YEMOJA:
So where is the Better Life for Rural Women in the city? (*YEMOJA goes into reflective silence while SHERIFAT briefly hums the tune of patience.*) But all the same, I am happy to be here and to see life here for myself. I see the challenge ahead of me and I must face it. Going back is a long tedious journey. Going forward is even longer. But you are here and I am here and that is what matters: that we are still here. Your words shake my feet. My feet are gathering strength. I can only move forward. I accept. I accept, mother Sherifat. My feet are burning. My lips are itching. I am ready. I want to sing! Sing! Sing! And dance for my people! Mother Sherifat. I am ready. Sing! My feet are ready to dance! (*SHERIFAT drums, drums and drums while YEMOJA dances and chants.*) I accept. I have come! I am here! Go tell the women! Tell the women of Idu that Yemoja has come and is here! Tell it to women when you return that I'm here where the soil burns but I still know my name. Tell them I am still Yemoja . . . handmaid of Onokwu/Yemoja, Sea Goddess and twin Goddess of the Earth! Tell the women that Yemoja lives. How can the Sea be afraid of time when she is the depth herself? How can she be afraid when she is God Herself? I am here! I am ready! Go tell it to women!

SHERIFAT:
Yes, Yemoja. Fear no modern women . . . no matter the sword of their pen. How can you fear when you bear the image of the God Herself? How can you fear the modern when you bear the voice of the ancient that shares boundaries with Earth? Daughter, you have

nothing to fear. Theirs is power passing in moments of time. But yours is the power of the land. Can anyone shift or move the land away from herself? No, daughter! Yours is the power of the spirit . . . power of the soul that is based on our earth, our land, our sea. How then can land be afraid of wind that passes in moments of time?

YEMOJA:

Yes. Winds will always blow and pass over. That is the nature of winds. But who can move the land away from source to plant winds?

SHERIFAT:

No! No! No! No one!

YEMOJA AND SHERIFAT: (*Together.*)

Who can? Who will move the land away from herself?

YEMOJA:

Mother, come. It is our time to dance, together . . . come. (*YEMOJA takes up her drum. Her fingers itch to beat the drum. She drums, drums again and takes a few quick steps toward the East. SHERIFAT follows. Drums take over until blackout.*)

MOVEMENT FOUR
Thunder Meets Fire

(*The living room. OKEI ties his shoelace as he prepares for work. He rises, walks over to the kitchen to get himself a can of juice from the refrigerator, and pours it into a glass as DAISY enters. She preens herself in front of the mirror that covers one end of the living room wall. She studies her behind. Satisfied, she strokes her false hair backward, flipping the extension braids in the manner of a Hollywood star in front of an audience. She seems to be temporarily carried away by this exotic image of herself; then OKEI breaks the silence.*)

OKEI: (*Adjusting his tie.*)
Well, I expect we all must go out and buy ourselves breakfast since it's no longer fashionable to be in the kitchen. And more so in this house, when it's now nobody's duty to even make arrangements for it. So eating out is the word. . . .

DAISY:
I guess that wouldn't be a bad idea at all. That should be a wonderfully welcome new code for our times. Eat out, and relieve women of the burden of cooking. And it's even more welcome if a fine man like you is ready to foot the bill. Who is Daisy to say no to such an angel of hosts? Man, I work hard for a living, and so do you, I suppose.

OKEI:
One of these days, someone is going to determine what codes are acceptable in this house and who pilots the ship. . . .

DAISY:
You won't have to look too far. After all, you've got two wonderful accomplices who pilot the ship for you already. Whatever you plan, your mother is there and so is your devotee, Yemoja, Empress of Gutters!

OKEI:
Just cut it out! Cut it out! Okay? This is a new day just beginning. I hope you will not ruin it with your terrorism. Everyone is now at risk with your new-found freedom and power: your children, your husband, your mother-in-law, your maid. . . . Except, of course,

(*emphatically*) "your Ruth," Her Holiness, the new Goddess of Feminism. It is incomprehensible to me that your new shero-cum-deitess-cum-empress cannot decide whether she wants to be man or woman. The name Ruth is the air we breathe in this house. We wake up to winds blowing the creed: feminism . . . feminism scented with the fine airs of her imperial majesty, Ruth the Rootless. With her new "ism" we get fed and bloated at breakfast, lunch and dinner. With what other food does the family need to get starved or constipated, if not FE-MI-NI-SM? Ugh! Ruth! The new goddess who goes about assaulting everyone's vision with her nudity in the name of emancipation and individual rights. I hope you know that the rest of us too have our own rights and, just like you, can exercise such rights. (*Silence.*) And you say you're going to work. See how you are dressed! Hawking your body on the streets and turning around to cry wolf about sexual abuse and sexual harassment and all that jazz. I'm fed up . . . completely fed up with women and complaints about sexual assaults, especially when the grapes go sour. You feminists are really incredible! You shout and scream rape each day. You shout that women are reduced to mere sex objects. See yourself! There's the mirror. Look critically at yourself and your vicious designs at being provocative and seductive, and tell me who should be complaining of sexual harassment: men or women? Woman, take a look at yourself again. Read what image you have unmade of woman! See for yourself what you have turned woman into: mere body! And at this point, I agree totally with Shakespeare's Hamlet: "God gave you one face but you found yourself another." Indeed I will add, for you modern women: "God gave you one face, and in your greed and pride, you reconstructed it until it collapsed." Now you have lost all face, woman! You now have neither grace nor wisdom. If a woman exposes her body as an object, what does she expect? I think it's high time someone made a case against the psychological abuse and sexual violence women inflict on mankind. Don't let me tell you, woman. . . .

DAISY:

It's your fantasy. All this talk about sexual abuse and violence is your calculated device to distort the image of women. And it all confirms our point about the malevolent myths men create about women.

OKEI:

Oh, Daisy stop! STOP! Not again! Not this morning! No! My system can't take that this early in the morning. I'm fed up. I'm fed up, woman! You're making my constitution weaker and weaker each day. I'm constipated with you, woman! And it's so unfair of you to feed your husband such garbage in place of breakfast this morning.

DAISY:

Well, your other women are there. You have Yemoja the "prefab" woman, imagined and preconditioned image of womanhood invented for your consumption. She's there to give you breakfast; that is, if your mother will let her. Your mother adores her, and so do you. And she'd rather obey you than me. *(Pause.)* Hmm . . . I do not know now who the enemy is: this other woman or my mother-in-law. But the interesting thing is that they are both in league with you against me. That should be a new, interesting dimension to feminist scholarship. . . .

OKEI:

Daisy, I can't understand you anymore. Can't you leave a tired man alone? Daisy, I'm on the ground, and I'm tired and begging. Let a man rest! Why must you keep pushing people around? Now you accuse me and my mother of being in league with Yemoja. The moment this same Yemoja arrived in this house, you told me she was directly under your control. You warned me never to interact directly with her! You instructed that every dealing with her must pass through you! That I understand, and I have kept to the letter! *(Pause.)* I'm also aware that you gave her the same warning. You created the boundaries. You've drawn many lines that she must not cross, including not taking initiative about when, or what, to cook. And now you, the same you, turn around and complain? You amaze me, woman! What is it that you want? *(Screaming.)* God, what do women want!! Can't you leave the poor rural woman alone? Why must you confuse her this way and burn her out in your new ego trip? Leave the rural woman alone!

DAISY:

Yes, I hear you, defender of the faithful. *(Mimicking OKEI.)* Leave the rural woman alone! I hear you! I know it's much easier to identify with her than with me. It's your purpose. It's your trick to keep women apart so you can continue to exploit them.

(At this moment, BOSE, the younger of their two daughters, comes down from the bedroom.)

BOSE:

Hi, Mummy and Daddy!

OKEI AND DAISY: *(Uneasy, but almost together.)*

Hi, Bose! *(OKEI is making more effort now to adjust his countenance to cover up his anger.)*

DAISY:
    You had a nice sleep?
BOSE:
    Yes, Mummy. . . .
OKEI: *(Thrusting his hand forward.)*
    Bose, come over here and give Daddy a hug. *(BOSE goes over to OKEI. He hugs her.)* That's my sweet girl! You slept well?
BOSE:
    Yes, Daddy . . . but . . .
OKEI:
    Any dreams last night?
BOSE:
    Hmm . . . no, Daddy! But . . .
OKEI:
    Great! That's my sweet babe! *(Brief silence.)* But what? Tell me!
BOSE: *(Looking at her mother.)*
    It took me a long time to fall asleep. I was so afraid last night. . . .
OKEI: *(Concerned.)*
    Why?
BOSE: *(Again looking at her mother.)*
    Oh . . . well . . . you see . . . Grandma Sherifat is here . . . and . . . and . . .
OKEI:
    And what?
DAISY: *(Cutting in.)*
    Perhaps Bose overheard our argument last night. . . .
OKEI:
    Why don't you let the child speak? Bose is a big girl now. She is ten years old. And I'm sure she can speak for herself! Bose, go on. What about Grandma Sherifat?
BOSE:
    Oh, Daddy, it's just nothing but, eh . . . but . . . what . . . eh . . . Mummy told me and Obianuju when Grandma visited here the last time.
OKEI:
    Hmm . . . and what was that? Tell me! Don't be afraid. Tell me what Mama said. What did your Mama say?
BOSE:
    That . . . that Grandma is a witch. . . .
OKEI:
    What?

BOSE:
> And . . . that we must be careful whenever she is here. We must watch her closely so she doesn't affect us with her voodoo. . . . (*OKEI studies DAISY for a while. DAISY is thoroughly embarrassed and begins to leave.*)

OKEI:
> I see. . . . (*Pause.*) What else did your Mama say?

BOSE:
> Mummy also says it's the reason why she doesn't allow us to go to the village. (*DAISY turns, facing BOSE threateningly.*)

DAISY:
> Now stop that, Bose! Why are you spinning all these tales this early in the morning instead of getting ready to go to school?

BOSE:
> I am waiting for Yemoja to find me the other pair of my school shoes!

DAISY:
> Well, go tell that Yemoja to find your shoes. . . .

OKEI:
> No, Daisy! (*He goes over to BOSE and holds her tenderly.*) My Bose is a big girl now and she can find her own shoes! Bose, are you not my lady?

BOSE:
> Yes, Daddy.

OKEI:
> Then go get your shoes, and quick, get ready for school! (*He kisses her, and BOSE runs off to get her shoes. While she's gone, OKEI quietly reflects, and DAISY paces, humming a tune to herself. Bose returns shortly.*)

DAISY:
> Now, Bose, go and eat your breakfast and go to school! (*BOSE walks toward the dining table.*)

BOSE:
> But, Mummy, you know breakfast is not ready yet. (*She turns to OKEI.*) Daddy, how am I going to learn at school without eating?

OKEI: (*Smiling.*)
> Ask your mother! (*In anger, DAISY rings the bell for YEMOJA. YEMOJA walks in, drying her hands with a napkin.*)

DAISY:
> Is breakfast ready yet?

YEMOJA:

I don't think so.

DAISY:

Why? What have you been doing?

YEMOJA:

I'm washing master's clothes and Bose's too. And I've been waiting for madam to tell me what to cook.

DAISY:

You're waiting for that, instead of doing what you are supposed to do? But you ought to know by now! You are not new in this house. And anyone with sense would have guessed the breakfast for this morning. Or don't you think so?

YEMOJA:

Madam, I don't "think so" because I am not allowed to . . . to . . . think. You asked me not to think. . . . (OKEI *begins to whistle and walks away from the women.*)

DAISY:

What?

YEMOJA:

Yes, madam. From the moment I came here, you asked me never to act on my own. You said I am only here to obey simple instructions. (DAISY, *shocked, stares at* OKEI. *Okei takes up his briefcase, ready to leave for work.* YEMOJA *exits.*)

DAISY: (*To* OKEI.)

Did you hear that?

OKEI: (*Cynically.*)

Well, I guess I did. But . . . Daisy, I'm just a man. I'm an outsider in this matter. . . . And you see . . . this early in the morning it's rather difficult to see . . . I mean . . . I wanted to say that I don't hear well at this time of the day. It's too early in the day to hear. . . .

DAISY:

Yes, that must be it. Your ears are dead and you're just as blind as you're dumb. Go on and mock yourself. Daisy will not yield her ground, not even to ten thousand of you, Okei. Go on and say nothing when your house is on fire.

OKEI: (*Laughing.*)

So my house is on fire? Who set it on fire, Daisy, tell me? Who set the house on fire? It would be nice to know. (*Silence.*) Hmm . . . well, I don't know what you expect me to say. I'm just an outsider. It's an issue between you and your fellow women. Isn't this a woman's world, as they say? And, I assume, under your control? I am only a man. What business has the vulture with a barber? You women can go and chew up one another or, better still, eat one another and stew in your own juice!! I'm off to work. *(He starts to leave. BOSE gives him a hug. While they embrace, DAISY walks across, takes her handbag, and marches toward the door, ready to leave.)*

DAISY:
I too am leaving, but I'm still waiting for someone to tell me what is going on in this house!

OKEI:
Amen! *(He pauses and turns to BOSE.)* Bose, you better hurry or you'll be late to school. *(He pulls BOSE closer to him. Daisy sighs and exits by the front door. She returns shortly and disappears into the bedroom.)* Now listen, you must stay close to sister Yemoja. . . . I want you to learn everything from her.

BOSE: *(Coldly.)*
From Yemoja?

OKEI:
Yes.

BOSE:
Hmm . . .

OKEI:
Why do you say "hmm" and you have that scowl on your face? What's wrong with learning from sister Yemoja?

BOSE: *(Still hesitating.)*
Hmm . . . nothing. Just that Mummy doesn't like Yemoja and . . .

OKEI:
Now, Bose. Don't mind what your Mama says.

BOSE:
I shouldn't mind what Mummy says?

OKEI: *(He is uneasy.)*
Oh, no! Not at all, Bose. I mean . . . Bose, all I'm saying is don't hate or disrespect anyone.

BOSE:
Even when Mummy says so?

OKEI:
Hmm . . . well, Bose. You must listen to your Daddy too. Daddy says it is not good for you to hate or disrespect anyone . . . because if you do, they too will hate you. *(He pulls her toward him tenderly and kisses her.)* And I'm sure my sweet one likes to be loved by everybody.

BOSE:

    What if Mummy tells me to hate someone again?

OKEI:

    Just tell her that Daddy says you have to show love to people for them to love you. Understand?

BOSE:

    Hmm . . .

OKEI:

    So, now you know. Yemoja is older. She's your sister by our tradition.

BOSE: *(Alarmed.)*

    Yemoja is my sister? Is she related to you or Mummy?

OKEI:

    Hmm . . . not exactly. But we are somewhat related. Everyone who comes from our place, Idu, is a brother or sister. It doesn't matter if we come from different families. We are all related. That is why, in Idu, we refer to one another as brother or sister. We never refer to one another as cousin or nephew or half-brother/half-sister or uncle. In Idu, there is no half-measure in sisterhood, in brotherhood or fatherhood.

BOSE:

    Why?

OKEI:

    Because that creates artificial distance between people. They would rather see one another as brother or sister to make people feel closer to one another.

BOSE:

    Hmm . . .

OKEI: *(He hugs her again.)*

    Don't worry, my "Lady B." There are so many things you do not know and need to know. But you will learn. You will learn. Sister Yemoja is here; so is Grandma, and so is Daddy. . . .

BOSE:

    And my Mummy too!

OKEI:

    Oh sure! Your Mummy is here too! *(OKEI begins to gather his things together, preparing to leave for work.)*

BOSE:

    Hmm . . . so Yemoja is my sister? I will . . . I have so many things to tell my friends . . . Jessica, Tammy and Titi at school. Daddy, did I tell you Titi's daddy is from Idu like you?

TELL IT TO WOMEN

OKEI:
No? He's from Idu like us? Then he's my brother too!

BOSE:
That I will tell Titi. I will tell her . . . that Yemoja too is from Idu.

OKEI:
Tell Titi sister Yemoja is from Idu. Tell her we are one. Call her "Sister Yemoja."

BOSE:
Sis . . . Sister . . . Ye-mo-ja . . . Sister Yemoja. Daddy, did I get it right?

OKEI:
Yes, my "Lady B." Got it! *(He kisses her.)* Call her "Sissy Yemoja" for short. And make sure you respect her too.

BOSE:
Daddy you always talk about respect. Why? And I'm to respect her and she's just our maid?

OKEI:
It doesn't matter what she or what anybody is: maid or gardener or janitor or governor. Just respect people. Learn to respect others. And especially if they're older than you are. And Sissy Yemoja has children. She's definitely much older than you. She could have been your mother, you know? So respect her. She's older than you are. Respect is very important in our tradition.

BOSE:
Our teacher said so too. So I know now that I should call all older women sister. What about Grandma? Should I also call her "Sissy"?

OKEI: *(Laughing.)*
No! No "Sissy" for Grandma. How can you call her "Sissy" when she's your Grandma?

BOSE:
So what do I call her then?

OKEI:
Grandma! She is your grandmother. Go to Sissy Yemoja now. We'll talk about it later. *(Enter Yemoja.)* Yemoja?

YEMOJA:
Brother, food . . . ?

OKEI:
I'm sure between you and Mama something will be worked out for Bose, and perhaps for the rest of us, to eat in this house. *(YEMOJA takes BOSE by the hand, but BOSE resists her.)* Now go get ready for school. And don't forget what you learn at home. It's all learning,

whether at home or at school. Now go, my sweetie. Bose, be a good girl now. I'll see you after school.

BOSE: *(Going out of the room with YEMOJA.)* Bye, Daddy! *(OKEI is at the door, about to leave, when RUTH walks in.)*

RUTH: Hi, Mr. Okei.

OKEI: Hi, Ms. Ruth.

RUTH: Is Daisy home? *(DAISY reenters, running frantically toward the door, only to see OKEI and RUTH at either side of the doorway.)* Strange . . .

DAISY: Well, you too can see for yourself. You didn't believe me when I called to tell you what I witnessed between these women this morning. And now the man. Ugh! *(She sighs.)* I tell you, Ruth, I am now a total stranger in this house. I don't know what is going on anymore. They've made me a total stranger in my own house! *(Her voice is shaky now.)* I . . . I . . . don't know what to do anymore. . . . I feel stigmatized. I wish I was never involved in all this campaign for women. I doubt if I can deal with this anymore.

RUTH: Oh come off it, Daisy! It's gonna be all right! Have faith in yourself, woman! How can you give up so soon? If you're not strong enough, you will then prove them right. Daisy, our enemies are strong. And that is why we must be stronger. Have faith in yourself. It's gonna be all right. And you gonna see who will smile at the end. The money has been approved by the government, and it's a huge sum too. You and I have a lot to gain from it, including a promotion. With faith on our side, the launching of the Better Life will succeed.

DAISY: Better Life for whom? For women like my mother-in-law? And this crab they call Yemoja?

RUTH: Why should we care? If the program succeeds after . . . after the launching, you and I will have made our gains. And that's what matters. You must never allow these backward women to discourage you and bring you down to their level. These villagers are a burden, and we must shake them off. They are endless burdens that you can't risk carrying on your head; you must carry them on your shoulder. Otherwise they'll bear you down forever. You gotta have guts and learn the game of life and play it cool. . . . We can't afford to lose now.

DAISY:

And Okei?

RUTH:

That shouldn't bother you either! He's just reacting like any man who thinks he's a king. And then suddenly this king is now bearing witness to the collapse of his kingdom, or rather empire. The empire is crumbling.... He may also be suffering from what I call "Womenopause." *(They both laugh.)*

DAISY:

Womenopause . . . ugh! Rather neat, Ruth. That's a new one! We must include that in Her Excellency's speech that we will prepare for her address at the launching. Her Excellency loves such catchy words.

RUTH:

Yeah! If they say aging women suffer from menopause, it's only logical that disempowered, aging men like your husband . . . my apologies . . .

DAISY:

Oh go on! No problem!

RUTH:

Yeah! Such men must suffer from "womenopause" *(Pause.)*

DAISY:

Great! *(She jots it down.)*

RUTH:

So what's up?

DAISY:

My mother-in-law! And that louse Yemoja! You were here when . . . I . . . poor me! I brought her in rags from the village. And now, after all the polish I've given her, she has the effrontery to talk back and weave all kinds of webs around me. If she doesn't leave this house this day with that old witch, they'll both know my name is not Daisy! I've already called for the driver from the minister's office to take them home, and I'm getting new guards, just in case.

RUTH:

Stop it! Come on, Daisy! *(Pause.)* You're making a very big mistake. You are getting paranoid! I'm sure we can win these women over. Consider how easy our mission was in the village. These rural woman are very gullible, you know. All you need to do is make them feel they are important. That's the magic! I'm sure it will work. And we need them anyway, maybe even more than they need us. Be patient and work hard at it. We need them to move the women along, and you know the women are coming soon. There is no time to waste. We must hasten with the arrangements. Write Her Excellency's speech, teach the women how to march, and then our new creed. There's so much ahead of us. Daisy, this is no time to despair.

DAISY:

I know . . . but that too is what I fear.

RUTH:

We mustn't allow things to slip through our fingers. Or we'll be a laughingstock before the men and these cynical "doubting Thomases." We must be ahead of the game always. You know men are tricksters and will use any device to win always. . . .

DAISY:

Not to mention losing my job. My job hangs on the success of this program. Both the minister and the president want to use this program to score political goals. If nothing else, it will go down in history as a positive image contribution devoted to the era of the UN Decade for Women.

RUTH:

And yesterday the aide-de-camp to the president's wife told me that Her Excellency's special outfit for the launching is already on display in her bedroom. I hear the fabric is the first of its kind. The outfit alone cost some 100,000 American dollars. It's made of coral and turquoise beads.

DAISY:

Waoo!! Well, what do you expect from one who insists on being called "First Lady"? First Lady my foot! She can't even spell her name!

RUTH:

Well, mind your language or be ready to spend the rest of your life in jail for blasphemy against Her Excellency. The First Lady who can't distinguish the letter "A" from the footprint of a cow! That's their business anyway. In the eyes of the world, Her Excellency is one of the most prolific authors who ever ruled. She's launched three books already.

DAISY:

Yeah! Books on how to be a wife . . . in the barracks . . .

RUTH:

She'll be launching a new one during the Better Life program. Full-time scholars like me are being paid to write books for Their Excellencies all over the world. The First Lady is only maintaining a modern tradition! It's her time.

DAISY:

    I understand that the president has made it compulsory for all government officials, ministers, commissioners and all important public figures to attend the launching.

RUTH:

    And you know what that means?

DAISY:

    Of course, that's lots of money from all the pockets for Her Excellency!

RUTH:

    Wao!

DAISY:

    And then another gimmick too!

RUTH:

    What's that?

DAISY:

    Her Excellency is receiving a "Grand Prix as the Champion of Rural Women." The news is still a closely guarded secret in official circles. It'll be their special national surprise at the launching of Better Life for Rural Women.

RUTH:

    Her Lady is making her day. Perhaps what we should be launching is the "Program of Better Women for Rural Life" instead of the "Program of Better Life for Rural Women! *(They laugh.)*

DAISY:

    As Nigerians say, which one concerns Agbero with overload? *(They laugh again.)*

RUTH:

    We are just obedient servants!

DAISY:

    Yeah, Your Excellency's obedient servants!

RUTH:

    Money changing hands!

DAISY:

    No! More like money returning to the source! The presidency awarded the money behind the scenes to some unknown international agency. Yeah, some unseen hand that looks a lot like Her Excellency's . . . smart!

RUTH:

    Arrangements are under way for worldwide satellite coverage of the launching, especially the BBC and the VOA.

DAISY:
>It's a battle of names for this occasions. Big names are going to collide.!

RUTH:
>And faces too!

DAISY:
>I must commission my own outfit.

RUTH:
>Well, the money is already built into the budget. Better use it while it lasts.

DAISY:
>Sure will!

RUTH:
>And make haste too while the "silk shines"! How about that for a new idiom of modernity? *(They both laugh.)* Rural women's representatives are here already.

DAISY:
>So the minister said. And the women met the ministry official for orientation today.

RUTH:
>What about Yemoja?

DAISY: *(She sighs.)*
>She's here. I don't know what to do with her now.

RUTH:
>Why, what do you mean? You brought her here for this program and now you say you don't know what to do with her? Put her to work. She's only a village woman! What does she know?

DAISY:
>Well, I hope we are not making an error. That woman is deep, deep like the sea. And now she's so close to my mother-in-law. Okei adores her too. What for, I cannot tell. I'm losing ground . . . everywhere. . . . Perhaps you can help me out.

RUTH:
>Oh, Daisy, don't despair. I've never known you to despair until now. What you are seeing is perhaps your husband's device to intimidate you. Your husband and mother-in-law are two of a kind. And your maid is another. Simpletons! Simpletons! (SHERIFAT *and* YEMOJA *have entered, but because* DAISY *and* RUTH *are so absorbed in their talk, they are not aware of their presence.*) That is what village women are!! Buy them with some nice presents and with some broad smiles. That's all. They'll follow. When you are done with them, dump

them. Your mission will have been accomplished and they won't know the difference when you use or dump them. Rural women are gullible. For now, prepare your mother-in-law and send them over to me for drills and orientation. And cheer up, dear. Everything will be all right. See you later. (RUTH *is kissing* DAISY *goodbye when* SHERIFAT *announces her presence with* YEMOJA. BOSE *is tagging behind.* SHERIFAT *carries a hanger with* BOSE's *dresses while* YEMOJA *carries* OKEI's *shirt. Shocked,* DAISY *pulls away from* RUTH. RUTH *is unruffled.*) See you, love. (*She leaves.*)

DAISY:
See . . . see you later. . . . (*Turning to* YEMOJA.) Ehm . . . ehm . . . Yemoja!

YEMOJA:
Yes!

DAISY: (*Cautiously now.*)
Ehm . . . from today you are to frequent the orientation program for the National Representatives of the Rural Women. Prepare immediately. Ruth is waiting outside for you. She is waiting to lead you there.

YEMOJA:
I see. And who is to cook the meal for the day?

SHERIFAT: (*Impatiently.*)
Yemoja, why do you cry louder than the owner of the corpse? If at last the powers think it is important for you to do what brought you here to the city, why don't you tie your wrapper tight and go? You were brought here, not bought.

YEMOJA:
I understand you, mother. But you know my concern.

SHERIFAT:
What is your concern? (*Pause.*) That the owner of the house and his daughter do not come and find the table empty? (DAISY *and* SHERIFAT *speak almost simultaneously.*)

DAISY:
What are you saying now, Yemoja?

SHERIFAT:
She didn't speak with water in her mouth, did she? Her concern is that my son and granddaughter will starve since there is no other "woman" in this house. Yemoja, go. I am here if no other woman is here. (*Silence.*)

DAISY:
Interesting . . . interesting development. (*Pause.*) I believe anyone in

doubt about who is the woman of this house needs to have her eyes checked. But that is not my concern now. Yemoja, leave immediately. Mama, it's time for you and I to talk. (*YEMOJA leaves the room.*)

SHERIFAT:
Talk? About what? I thought some of us were too low for the mighty ones!

DAISY: (*Trying to control her anger, but coaxing her all the same.*)
Oh, Mama! You take things rather too seriously! I can see you've not forgotten what happened when you arrived. . . .

SHERIFAT:
Yes, I remember! But as they say, it's easier for the ones who inflict the pain on others to forget.

DAISY:
Well, I can see you're hurt. But I didn't mean it that way.

SHERIFAT:
Whichever way you meant it, it doesn't matter. Nothing matters anymore.

DAISY:
Okay, Mama. Let's put that episode behind us and move forward. How are the women in the village?

SHERIFAT: (*Tersely.*)
They were doing well when I left them.

DAISY:
And how are they preparing for the launching?

SHERIFAT:
Of what?

DAISY:
The Better Life program. (*Pause.*) I thought that was why you came to the city.

SHERIFAT:
I thought so too . . . until I saw the city.

DAISY:
I know it's different, Mama. But the city too has its own enchantments. The city has its glamor, which our women have been denied for ages just because they are so distant from it. We are committed to equality and justice. And we have made it our duty to bring our rural women to share in the glory of the city; to liberate them from the oppressive claws of tradition, from husbands and from the nightmare of childbearing. . . .

SHERIFAT:
Yes, I can see that. No one needs a lantern to see what your vision is.

Daisy:
That is our commitment . . . to show light to the women.

Sherifat:
And do you think they are blind?

Daisy:
Certainly not! But the Better Life program offers them a new opportunity for independence and the delights of life. For example, when the women arrive, they will be lodged in the Sheraton Hotel, one of the most expensive five-star hotels in the world.

Sherifat:
For five days?

Daisy:
Yes, for the entire week they will be here. The women will have access to the best meals, the best facilities, swimming pools, live bands every night, chauffeur-driven buses, room service for meals if they so desire, hot or cold bath, whatever they prefer. Air conditioning, and oh, name it. Anything that can make life joyful, without sweat. . . .

Sherifat:
For one week?

Daisy:
Yes, a new beginning! A new key in the hands of women to open the doors of life!

Sherifat:
I see. . . . (*Yemoja walks back in.*) Yemoja, our daughter, did you hear our women will be in a big hotel?

Yemoja:
Is that so?

Sherifat:
May we live to see the changes, my daughter!

Yemoja:
I'm ready. (*Daisy goes to check the wall clock.*)

Sherifat: (*Blessing her.*)
Go well, my daughter! May our ancestors walk before and behind you! You are the alligator pepper for daughters of Idu! Alligator pepper never goes on a shameful mission!

Daisy:
Hurry up, Yemoja! The women must be waiting for you!

Yemoja:
They won't have to wait much longer now. I'm on my way. See you soon.

DAISY:
> See you later. (Exit YEMOJA.)

SHERIFAT:
> And you say "Gomenti" is paying for all this?

DAISY: (Excitedly.)
> Oh, certainly! The government is very glad to do all this.

SHERIFAT:
> Why? What do they stand to gain? (Silence.) I do not trust these people. We, the daughters of Idu, also know "Gomenti." When "Gomenti" is not a chameleon, changing colors to suit its purpose, it is a rat biting you and blowing air into the sores to soothe the pain. We have not forgotten all they did to us in the last election. They made so many promises. They even brought water pipes and poles to show us they meant what they said. What happened to us after the election? The same "Gomenti" came to remove the water pipes and poles after we voted, because they lost the election. Idu remembers this. And that is why we daughters of Idu must dance with caution. "Gomenti" is a soldier. How can a woman love a soldier without the fear of death? And I tell you, every daughter of Idu knows that people in "Gomenti" never give a present without wanting something in return. We are aware of that. That is why they sent me here, because Yemoja is just one woman and she is still young.

DAISY:
> I see you people have thought about this. But we too are your daughters. We are in government to speak for you.

SHERIFAT:
> So you say. Our eyes are not closed even though we may appear to be asleep.

DAISY:
> As soon as Yemoja returns, we'll show you the marching step that you'll teach the women when they arrive.

SHERIFAT:
> I hear you.

DAISY: (Excitedly.)
> Good! That's important! We must come together. We must work together . . . you, I, all of us! But we must organize. . . . The women are coming. . . . (Suddenly they hear the sound of footsteps running toward them. It is BOSE. She is panting now.)

BOSE:
> Mummy! Mummy! I forgot . . .

DAISY: (Impatiently.)
> What?

BOSE: *(Still panting.)*
>Titi called to invite me over to her house.

DAISY:
>Hmm...

BOSE:
>It's about the assignment....

DAISY:
>What assignment now, Bose?

BOSE:
>But I told you before. It's our class project on culture. Titi and I chose to work on Idu, since we're from there. Not so, Mummy?

DAISY:
>Hmm... yes....

BOSE:
>Titi's mother knows a whole lot about the people, and she's going to tell us a whole lot about them... eh... our people.... I mean her mother is going to tell us about the traditions of our people.... I'm so happy, Mummy! My project is going to be the best in class! I'll get information from Titi's mummy and add that to what Grandma and Sissy Yemoja told me.... Oh, Mummy, it's so interesting. They told me so much... they're giving so much....

SHERIFAT: *(Sarcastically.)*
>Hmm... I can see that, my learned one. I see that you learn so much that you forget to greet your elders.... Or is respect for people not the very root of what I taught you about our customs?
>... *(Before she has finished this statement, BOSE is already down at the feet of her grandmother.)*

BOSE: *(Greeting.)*
>"Ojogwu," Nne! *(SHERIFAT holds up her right hand and places it on BOSE's head affectionately, chanting praise names of their lineage.)*

SHERIFAT:
>Daughter of Idu! Daughter of Idigwu, God of Iron... Umuozu, eaters of fire! People who can carry fire on their palms and still smile their way through life! Daughter of Idu! Master craftsmen and women. Weavers and blacksmiths. Owners of skillful hands that cast and carve and mold...! Arise... my daughter! May you live to nurse Idu. May Idu live to nurse you!

BOSE: *(Rising.)*
>Issseeeh! *(SHERIFAT helps her to dust her knees as DAISY watches rather impatiently because of the delay this ritual is causing.)*

SHERIFAT: *(Sensing DAISY's discomfiture.)*
>Well, I don't know what you women nowadays teach your young

ones. And I don't know what the teachers teach them in school either. What form of education is greater than knowing your way of life and where you come from? And who should know this best but you mothers? What do teachers know about our customs? I tell you, they may know all the customs about white people whose language they speak; but they are not part of us, and do not know us. I doubt that you know either.

DAISY:

But your world is different. . . .

SHERIFAT:

Wait, let me finish. . . . (DAISY, *sensing an argument, pushes* BOSE *gently away to avoid further trouble.*)

DAISY:

Bose, leave us now. Go where you want to go.

BOSE: (*Excitedly.*)

Bye, Mummy! (*Walking over to* SHERIFAT.) Grandma . . . I'll be back to see you and Sissy Yemoja, so . . .

DAISY: (*Impatiently.*)

Bose, go now! Time is running out!

BOSE: (*Leaving hurriedly.*)

Okay, Mummy! (*Exit* BOSE. *Brief silence.* DAISY *is deep in thought.*)

SHERIFAT:

Hmm . . . and that reminds me. . . . (*Pause.*) I can't understand you women of nowadays. What are you waiting for?

DAISY: (*Startled.*)

Hmm? What did you say?

SHERIFAT:

I say what are you waiting for?

DAISY:

Like what?

SHERIFAT:

Well, if you want me to name it. But all I can say is that I do not understand you women of nowadays. Bose is ten years old. She is almost a woman. And she is the last of two daughters. . . .

DAISY:

Hmm . . . I know that.

SHERIFAT:

Well, you know. And what are you doing about it? Is it not time for you to have another child? Or is it when the sun sets that you will begin to think of that? Look! The life of a woman is like that of a tree. A tree bears flowers and fruit. Each tree has its own season. No tree bears forever, you know. So what are you waiting for?

DAISY:
I'm not waiting for anything. I have two children. I'm done. It's my life and nobody else's. And it has got nothing to do with anyone else or any tradition. It's my business. It's my life.

SHERIFAT:
What do you mean it's your life? It's my life too!

DAISY:
Your life is my life? What do you mean? What are you telling me?

SHERIFAT:
That my son's wife should not break the links in the chain.

DAISY:
What link? What chain are you talking about?

SHERIFAT:
Many links! Many chains! Eternal links, Daazi. Your eyes may be open to white man's ways, but I tell you, you're still blind to our ways. It's not just a matter of having children.

DAISY:
But what's it about, then?

SHERIFAT:
About continuity! About life here and hereafter! Your children are the branches of your soul! Of the eternal cord that binds us to one another: here, now, before, after, and onto Earth. Can't you see? If I were you, I would go closer to my mother and ask her to tell me what tune matters in these parts, my "Oyibo woman." Ask your mother what it means not to have a child at all, or not to have a male child for that matter. . . .

DAISY: *(Interrupting.)*
I can't buy a male child! I take what nature offers me. . . .

SHERIFAT:
It is not a question of buying.

DAISY:
But of what?

SHERIFAT:
But of understanding. . . . I mean our way of seeing life and seeing the world. It's about . . . it is a question of identity!! Identity, Daazi!

DAISY:
You mean it's only the male child who determines issues of identity? Must identity only be seen by way of the male? Where do you place the female?

SHERIFAT: *(Laughing.)*
Hey, you really amuse me! Nobody says a female child is nothing! Who can say that? Am I not a woman? Are you not a woman? But think of it. Think of us. . . . Are you in your father's home now? Am I in my father's home now? *(Brief silence.)* This is what we must accept. Every tree needs to have solid roots in order to survive and stand. Every tree needs its own branches to grow. A tree which bears no fruit, that will in turn bear its own kind of seed, is dead and is soon cut down and carted away for firewood. Every tree bears its own kind. The oil bean tree bears its own pods that must dry and disperse to the seven winds. Daughters are of immense value. Isn't it our people who name their daughters Nwanyibueze? (The female is supreme.) Nnebueze? (Mother is supreme.) Nwayibuife? (The female is something precious.) But the same people also name their sons Okeibunor. (A male child is the root of the homestead.) A son is the root of the family. Why do you think they say all these things in one breath? It's our many ways of seeing the world. Not just one way. It's not this, or that, like you Oyibo people. We see the world in circles: the male is male, and the female is female. No one can take the place of another; no one is greater than another. Their value is not measured in terms of greater or lesser value. Each one is priceless in the order of things. Each one is part of the other, male and female. It is not a matter of male or female. . . .

DAISY:
But of what?

SHERIFAT:
It is the fact of our being. . . . The female child is born of value. Like the oil bean seed, she must be dispersed to sprout and branch out elsewhere. But the root, borne from the seed . . . the parent tree must survive. What happens if the seed disperses and cannot take root?

DAISY:
That is clear! That is a risky venture. To begin with, every venture has its own risks. And I've yet to comprehend your obsession with men. . . .

SHERIFAT:
Ha! Ha! Ha! For men? It's not that simple, my child! A female child is a female child. And a male child is a male child. Maize cannot take the place of yam in the cooking pot. And yam cannot take the place of maize. . . . Each one has its own place and value in the barn. . . . And don't you know the saying among our people? A female child is like a bird. A bird may not know other lands, but it journeys

there all the same! (*Sherifat begins to sing the song.*) Ije enu bu afia-o Afia baa li onye ozua-o Nwa okporo bu egbe-o Egbe amali ani ogaa! Nwa okoro bu egbe-o Egbe amali ani ogaa! Ije enu bu afia Afia baali onya ozua.... (*Translation of song: Life is a marketplace. If the market is good, you profit. If the market is bad, you lose. A female child is like a bird. The bird does not know other lands but journeys there all the same. The world is a marketplace. If business is good, you profit. If business is bad you lose. The female child is a bird which sets out on a journey to a foreign land not knowing the ways of that land. What she takes out of that land depends on her fortune and willpower. But go on the journey, she must. For the journey is her life! For the journey is our life! For the mission is her life!*) (*Sherifat is still singing when Ruth storms in through the doorway. Sherifat stops. Daisy turns to Ruth, whose hand is still on the door. Brief silence. Ruth, sensing some awkwardness, asks.*)

RUTH:
Ehn ... well, did I interrupt something?

DAISY: (*Trying to gather her thoughts.*)
Hmm ... no! Not really. No, Ruth!

RUTH: (*Entering and sitting down.*)
Hmm ... interesting. (*Sherifat departs.*) Good day, Mrs. Nweke!

SHERIFAT:
Good day to you, "Lutu." How are your children and husband?

RUTH:
Hmm ... that's a nice one.... I don't have a husband. I don't have children either.

SHERIFAT: (*Alarmed.*)
What? What are you waiting for?

RUTH:
What am I waiting for? Nothing! Absolutely nothing!

SHERIFAT:
At your age? Don't you know the saying among our people?

RUTH:
What? What saying?

SHERIFAT:
If the market rejects you, do not reject yourself.

RUTH:
How do I relate to that in these times?

SHERIFAT:
If you can't find a husband who will make you pregnant, by all means bear a child in your father's name! (*Before she completes the*

statement, RUTH has burst into the kind of laughter that indicates she's mocking SHERIFAT's statement. SHERIFAT is completely scandalized.)

RUTH:
You people really amuse me! You mean a woman must go to such a ridiculous extent just to breed babies? (*DAISY, sensing that this might become explosive, gets up and begins to pat RUTH's hand, signaling her to be quiet. But RUTH is determined to make her point.*) I can't understand where you mothers are coming from.

SHERIFAT:
I can't understand where you wild women are going!

DAISY:
Hey, Ruth! Cut it out....

RUTH:
Hey, girl! Let it flow! I gotta tell it to the ... these ...

DAISY:
No, girl! It's bad timing! There will ... there will be time to tell ...

RUTH: (*Petulantly.*)
No, Daisy! I can't ... wait ... any more! I'm ... I'm ... I'm choking ... choking from all the stuff and nonsense....

DAISY: (*Still trying to stop RUTH.*)
Ruuuuuuuth!! Not now!

RUTH:
Hey, leave me alone! I gotta tell ... tell it to the ... these ... primitive vestiges of womanhood who call themselves mothers! You gotta show them their place ... these dwellers of the zoo, sentenced to life in motherhood and mothering! And yet, not knowing the difference. They delude themselves with their imagined empowerment through spiritual elevation and social mobility. And totally oblivious to their imprisonment to life, tradition. Don't let me tell you women!

SHERIFAT: (*Mocking laughter.*)
Ha! You want to tell? Tell! Go on and tell! Tell it! Tell it! Tell it to us! Tell us where our Chi has branded us and destined us to stay grounded on earth while you fly like chickens chasing after hawks in the air! (*At this moment, when the air is so charged and tense, OKEI enters.*) Go on! Tell it! Tell us we lack wings and we cannot fly! But remember, my learned one, not all animals have wings. Not all animals fly, my learned one! The tortoise may not fly, but her wisdom empowers her to soar above the eagle. The monkey may not have wings, but she too flies in the air, competing for heights with the eagle. In life, my learned one, you do not always have wings to fly.

The modern hen may mask her pain of life in glittering lashes and feathers, but this chicken too sweats . . . she sweats, beneath her feathers. . . . The monkey may wear a tail, but she may show more dignity than the new brands of women. . . . My learned one, the monkey too has her own beauty! Or what do you think she does when she glides through the air? Does she borrow your massive buttocks to make her fly? No, my learned one! (*SHERIFAT has become so carried away now that she glows and chants in celebration, while RUTH watches her in utter disgust, and DAISY looks on with a mixture of scorn and awe.*)

SHERIFAT:

I can show you life in these lines, etching the rhythms of seasons on my palm. . . . Each one his own, each one her own. Each one with its own peculiar powers and mastery of nature to make it conquer, survive and be in tune with its own rhythm of life. Go on! Tell it, my learned one! Tell us that we are handicapped. But I tell you, the destiny of the hen is not the destiny of the cock!! Each one, its own season; each one, its own reason. Note these as you tell and blow our loin cloths open in the wind. Go on and tell!! Tell us that we are blind because we cannot read and write! Tell it! Tell the women we are poor! But I tell you, my Oyibo, my learned one, it will take the likes of you ten more generations to understand what the rural woman knows about life. It will take you ten lifetimes to comprehend the simple language of breeze to leaves, as the sun is waking up. Or even the salute of the flashes that tell and show the mood of the Earth, our mother in her eternal dialogue with us, her children. My learned one, it will take you another life to distinguish the difference between the sky's loud laughter and his growl which soon breaks into tears that drench humanity, old and young, rich and poor. My learned one, it will take you another life to tell the difference between the sad song of leaves turning yellow and singing their pain as they await the harmattan season from their joyous chorus when their chests begin to shoot forward young, delicate nipples suckled by gentle winds wooing and flirting with their eternal suitors, sun and rain in the ever-seductive dance of life. The dance that gives birth to death . . . the acrobatic dance of death that swirls to life. Hey, my learned woman! What do you know about life? What do you know about being woman who is born and bred and buttered and battered in the soul and rhythm of ages and seasons that the rural woman does not know? What do you know about woman? If you would listen, I could tell you the true colors of woman! If you would come down from your throne mounted in air, I could show you the character of the land changing in texture as earth and soil dance, after rain and sun affirm their union until their multiple joys swell the chest of our Earth to abundant harvests. Oh, my learned woman! I could tell you how my spirit hears and sings the music of the land with my feet, charting her changing voices from season to season. Oh, my learned woman! I could! I could tell! Tell you what the moon says to the sun in their nocturnal meetings. I could tell you why the sun woos the moon; why the moon needs the sun . . . and why both need each other . . . complement each other and are never measured in terms of equality. Each one, its beauty. Each one, its own glow of fire . . . tinged with shades of fear! The moon sails the sky! So does the sun! But they seek each other, flirt and fight with each other until one bows to the other, and the other bows to it, my learned one. We do not see these bows in terms of conquests, but triumphs in the consummation of life and nature. Or what do you think the moon does when she disappears into the dark of the sky? You think she sleeps till the many fingers of sun poke her to wakefulness again? You think she snores while the many phalluses of suns stroke and rouse her to laughter? Or do you think she is silent? No, my learned one! The moon appears silent so that through her, the world may live; that through her, the earth may be born; that through her constant deaths and waking and sleeping and smiling, woman may plot the rhythm of being. Who knows the character of moon but us? The moon swoons, our womb showers! The moon weeps, our womb floods. The moon smiles, our womb swells! Oh, my learned one! I could tell you about being, and being woman in season and out of season. For I am woman and the moon is a character in my life! Oh, my learned one, don't let me tell you!

RUTH: *(Blocking her ears and screaming at the same time.)*
ENOUGH!! *(In anger, RUTH flings her files into the air, and DAISY, afraid of her next move, tries to come between Ruth and her mother-in-law. Suddenly OKEI coughs. Potent silence. The uneasy silence continues until DAISY, in her embarrassment, gathers strength to say something. DAISY stammers and tries to draw RUTH's attention to OKEI's presence.)*

DAISY:
Ehm . . . em . . . Ru . . . loo . . . look who's here. . . . *(RUTH turns, sees OKEI and slowly elbows her way into DAISY's supporting arms, but DAISY too is shaky and squirms her body out of Ruth's arms. RUTH gasps and starts sputtering. At that moment SHERIFAT turns her back on them, walking away and beginning to hum her earlier tune about the life journeys of women. OKEI too smiles knowingly and walks toward the stairs as he unknots his tie.)*

RUTH:
>I'm choking! (*DAISY, trying hard to ease the tension, now holds RUTH tenderly.*)

DAISY: (*Rummaging through her handbag.*)
>Ehm . . . Ruth . . . I'll show you! (*She finds the object of her search and waves it in the air.*) Look, Ruth! See! I've got fine news for you. . . . Ehm, ehm . . . it's a letter from the president! Grant for our launching! I'm expecting the minister's call for us to collect the money at any moment now. . . . (*RUTH is still lost in thought. SHERIFAT is now alert to what DAISY is saying and turns around. DAISY becomes silent temporarily, then, in a cajoling manner, says to SHERIFAT.*)

DAISY:
>Okay, Mama. Wee . . . we'll learn. It will soon be over. But . . . but for now, leave us alone. (*Turning to RUTH.*) Okay, girl! We'll be leaving. . . . (*As DAISY is talking, OKEI reenters the living room. The phone rings. He is nearer to the phone than she. He stretches his hand to pick it up, but DAISY jumps up at the same time to get it.*)

OKEI:
>That's my call!

DAISY:
>No! It's mine!

OKEI:
>I'm expecting a call from His Excellency. . . .

DAISY:
>I, too, am expecting a call from His Excellency! (*The phone rings again. The couple now locks horns over who will answer the telephone. SHERIFAT observes what is going on.*)

OKEI:
>Leave the telephone, woman!

DAISY:
>Leave the telephone, man! (*Phone continues to ring. DAISY positions herself threateningly by the phone. Phone rings again and again.*)

OKEI: (*Sighing and giving way.*)
>Okay. You win!

DAISY: (*Ignoring him and picking up the phone.*)
>Hello? (*OKEI stands watching her in disdain. SHERIFAT pulls him by the right hand.*)

SHERIFAT:
>Come, my son. Leave them alone. . . . (*They leave.*)

DAISY:
>Hmm . . . yeah. . . . May I know who's calling? Assistant to the

Minister for Transportation . . . hmm . . . yeeesss! Yeah! Yes, speaking! I'm the Director for Women's Affairs. Pardon? What did you say? . . . The women? The women are where? HERE? . . . THE WOMEN ARE HERE? My GOD! I'm doomed! The women are here? Where? Here! My God!! Bye!! (*DAISY drops the phone and throws herself on RUTH's shoulder, sobbing.*)

RUTH: (*Concerned.*)
What?

DAISY: (*Sobbing.*)
The women are here . . . and . . . eh . . . I . . . we are not ready! These women will be my ruin!

RUTH: (*Collecting herself.*)
Now stop it, Daisy! What is happening to you? Where's your power gone? Why is your courage failing you for these mere bush women? Get the pieces of yourself together, babe, and let's plan. Why do you think I'm here?

DAISY: (*Tearfully.*)
I know, but I'm . . . I'm afraid now that everything is so near. Oh, Ruth! What will I do? I'm so afraid of failing. We're responsible for everything. The world knows that and everyone holds us responsible. And if . . . if . . . we fail?

RUTH:
Well, you're the Director of Women's Affairs, not me. . . . Eh . . . I mean . . . we . . . we're in this thing together. But one can only do so much and hope for the best. My role in this whole process is to help create a viable atmosphere for the empowerment of women. That's why I'm involved: to research women's development in this region and publish the reports afterward. The world knows who's responsible, except no one can claim innocence in the matter. . . .

DAISY:
What the hell are you talking about? You too will abandon me?

RUTH:
Certainly not! I'll be with you . . . till the end. Isn't it obvious we're in this together? Let's not waste time on frivolous arguments now. We must get going. . . . The women are here. . . . (*OKEI reenters.*)

DAISY: (*Going over to him.*)
Okei . . . the women are here. . . .

OKEI: (*Arrogantly.*)
So I hear! You asked for it. What's your problem?

DAISY: (*Defensively.*)
Well, there's no problem. . . . I . . . ehm . . . I just wanted to ask you eh . . . em . . . for a favor. . . .

OKEI: *(Laughing.)*

A favor! For whom? Woman? To man? My God! I hope I'm safe! Come see me, see trouble! What business has the vulture with a barber? What else do you need, woman? You have it all . . . you got it all! I thought you had the world under your control!

(OKEI begins to whistle gleefully and exits.)

RUTH:

I've told you, Daisy. Leave him alone! I can't understand. You're so panicky. Let him go his way, please. *(Pause.)* Okay! So it's our own business. Everything is under control between me and Daisy. All responsibilities will be shared. And we're all equal to . . .

DAISY:

No, Ruth! You don't understand! You've forgotten that the women are many and are here already. Everything is strange here, and we need someone to guide them. . . .

RUTH:

No problem! Put your mother-in-law and Yemoja to work! That is why they are here in the first place. And they know the women better too. So what's the problem? Stay cool, babe . . . everything is coming together.

(YEMOJA returns.)

DAISY:

And see, Yemoja is back already. I know it will soon be over. By the way, what about the check from the government? Did you cash it as agreed?

RUTH:

Of course! It's breathing safe in the bank.

DAISY:

Great! Now all we need is just enough to manage these goats here. You got that?

RUTH:

Trust me! *(They laugh.)*

DAISY:

Prepare the women in the basement about what to do.

RUTH:

What?

DAISY:

Go tell the women . . . *(Suddenly the door opens. BOSE is back home.)*

BOSE: *(Excitedly.)*

Oh, Mummy! I got so much to tell . . . I've been learning so much.

DAISY: *(Trying to stop her.)*
    Bose, you are back!

BOSE:
    Yes, Mummy! Mummy! The program is great!

DAISY:
    Yeah, I know that, Bose. It's great. But you must leave me now.

BOSE:
    But . . . but, Mummy! I want to tell . . .

DAISY:
    Oh, this child! *(Screaming.)* BOOOOSEEE!!

BOSE: *(Hurt.)*
    Mummy . . . Mummy . . . but . . . I wanted to tell you . . .

DAISY: *(Now holding her tenderly.)*
    No, Bose! No, babe . . . not today . . . not now! Not now! Tell it later. Leave it for . . . tomorrow. . . .

BOSE:
    Mum . . . Mummy . . . but . . .

DAISY: *(Calmly and resignedly.)*
    Just hold it, babe! There will be time . . . time . . . time to tell your story. . . .

BOSE:
    But . . . but . . . when will it be time, Mummy?

DAISY:
    Not now . . . not now babe. Not now. Now go to bed. . . .

BOSE:
    Mummy, it's not night yet. I don't feel sleepy.

DAISY: *(Losing her temper again.)*
    My God! Save me from this child! Or have they sent you to kill me too? Bose, won't you listen to your own mother? *(It is clear that BOSE is peeved, and she begins to sulk.)*

RUTH:
    Bose, will you listen to what your Mama says?

BOSE:
    I want to . . . I will. . . . *(BOSE breaks down, sobbing freely now. SHERIFAT hears her and reenters, running to her rescue along with YEMOJA. RUTH gives them a nasty glance and starts walking toward the door.)* Why must I listen to Mama always? Mama never listens to me! Why must I listen to Mama all the time?

DAISY: *(Embarrassed and attempting to be gentle.)*
    Okay, child, I'm here. I hear you. I'll listen. For now, go . . . to bed.

... (*She notices* YEMOJA *and* SHERIFAT. *Pauses.*) Em, eh, yes, my good babe. I will ... I will.... (*Motioning to* YEMOJA.) Now, there's Yemoja. Go with Yemoja.... (YEMOJA *is already bending down to lift* BOSE *while* SHERIFAT *wipes away the tears from* BOSE's *brow*. RUTH *exits.*)

SHERIFAT: (*Briefly humming an ancient lullaby to* BOSE.)

Why do you cry, my child, when your Mama is here? Who beat my child?

DAISY:

Nobody beat her! She's just being naughty!

BOSE: (*Protesting.*)

It's not true, Grandma! Mummy is always picking on me! (DAISY *gives* BOSE *an uncharitable look and goes upstairs into the bedroom while* BOSE *sobs freely in* SHERIFAT's *arms.* SHERIFAT *continues to wipe away her tears and soon begins a praise chant to soothe* BOSE.)

SHERIFAT:

Who beats a daughter of Idu? A mere woman, for whom my son paid with my own money, beats my own daughter? Nooo! You're greater than every woman, my daughter! Or do you want me to take her case to the daughters of the clan? Umuada? You remember what I told you? (BOSE *nods.*) Ehem! That is a true daughter of Idu! (*Handing her over to* YEMOJA.) See? See, Yemoja? That is my daughter! (YEMOJA *cuddles* BOSE. *Soon,* YEMOJA *joins* SHERIFAT *in chanting the eulogy.*)

SHERIFAT AND YEMOJA:

Don't you cry. Your Mama lives, my child! Don't you cry! Daughter of Ogwugwu, God of iron! Ojogwu! Umuozu! Owners of hands skilled in bending metals! Umuozu! Omenka! Great weavers, craftsmen and women who outshine and outlast them all! Daughter of Omenka! Great women who weave intricate patterns of life with fingers of bone. Ojogwu! Ede! Daughter of thunder! Clan of sons and daughters whose voices send adversaries crashing to the ground! Dooooh, my child! Diji! Master farmers! Owners of the land who harvest the hugest yams! Daughter of Diji Ogbunganaba! Those who bear yams that fill both arms! Nwadike! Master wrestlers whose backs never see the earth in the wrestling arena! Mkpisiakanete-lege-lege: mbosi ogu osia lim ike! I salute you, fingers that look frail but flash with fire on the day of battle! (YEMOJA *departs abruptly but soon returns, and gently begins to beat the drum while* SHERIFAT *continues her praise chants to* BOSE.)

SHERIFAT:

So who dares touch my own? Who dares touch my daughter ... my own daughter? My husband! Ajie, my mother! How can my mother be crying before her children? You remember what Mama said? (*Bose is silent now.*) You're the image of my mother! You are my mother come back to life. And mama was a great mother! Mama was a great woman! So how can you cry before the chaff of women? Don't you cry! Don't you cry, my daughter! Mama is here! Mama is here! No more tears, no more tears, my child. Mama is here! Mama is here with you! Come into Mama's arms . . . (*Bose's mood has changed, and now she joyously jumps into her grandmother's arms. Sherifat almost drops her as she jumps, but she begins to chant.*) No! Ogwugwu forbids! How can you fall? How can my child fall when my arms are still strong and I am wide awake? No, my panther! The step of the hen never kills her chicks. Rain never beats on the vulture in its own nest! I am here! Ugo . . . my eagle . . . beauty of the birds! Your mother is here! Don't mind those who abuse you. They'll answer for what they do to you. . . . (*Daisy enters. The drums go silent. The women stop.*)

DAISY:

What's going on here? Bose, why are you still here? Won't you go to bed?

BOSE:

I'm not sleepy. (*Silence.*)

DAISY:

And did you eat yet? (*Before Bose can respond, Daisy turns vehemently to Yemoja.*) Yemoja, what have you been doing? This child is starving! And it's time for her to rest. But you stand there chattering and disturbing decent people who want peace. . . . Why have you not fed Bose yet? Or isn't it time? (*Before she finishes her last sentence, Bose is already responding.*)

BOSE:

It's not bedtime yet! And I want to hear Grandma and Sissy . . .

DAISY: (*Petulantly.*)

Sissy? Sissy what? (*Brief silence.*)

BOSE:

Sissy Yemoja! She tells me folktales . . . she and Grandma. . . . I love the folktales. . . .

DAISY:

You too? My own child that I carried for nine endless months in my own womb? (*She goes into a tantrum and, in her exasperation, pulls off a shoe, throws it at Bose and barely misses her head. Her anger now has free rein.*) Stop the nonsense! STOP! Now go and get your meal. Stop feeding me with trash! I'm fed up! Fed up and tired! What the hell are all of you turning my house into? Nonsense! All I hear from everyone is utter nonsense! Nonsense! And abuse! Abuse! From my own child! From husband! From maid! From countless tribes of in-laws! (*She attempts to pounce on* BOSE, *but the other women are between them, and* YEMOJA *quickly uses her body to shield* BOSE *against* DAISY's *descending arm.* DAISY *is still determined to break through the women and grab* BOSE *when* SHERIFAT *violently pushes her away.*)

SHERIFAT:
How dare you attempt to strike a child who is under another's protection? Did those who taught you ever say anything to you about morals? (*Silence.* DAISY's *fierce arm has frozen in the air, and she now pants with subdued rage.* OKEI *returns.* BOSE, *looking frightened, is now shivering but controlled inside the broad embrace of* YEMOJA, *who has now tucked her into her bosom. Brief silence.*)

OKEI:
What the hell's going on in this house! (*Silence.*) Won't nobody talk? What is going on?

SHERIFAT: (*Slowly picking her words.*)
Ask your wife.

DAISY:
Ask your mother! (OKEI *looks from his mother to* DAISY *and from* DAISY *to his mother again and then at* YEMOJA, *sitting on the floor with the child sobbing in her arms. He takes a deep breath and then goes to stand between his wife and his mother.*)

OKEI:
So nobody will tell me what's going on? (*Silence. He sighs.*) Nobody talks to me now because I have become a total stranger in my own house. House! House! That's all I have now! The home is gone! I go to work, I cannot concentrate. I come home, I cannot sit still. When I come in here, nobody recognizes me anymore!

DAISY: (*Sarcastically.*)
Maybe you'll do yourself a favor and wear a name tag or label to be recognized here.... (*Before she completes the statement,* OKEI *has flared up into an uncontrollable rage.*)

OKEI:
Yes, go on and destroy the home! Quick! Destroy it! And don't stop until the whole edifice has crumbled! Go on and set the family ablaze! And the ashes? Use them to powder your face ... or indeed, sell them to make a profit for yourself! Self! That's all you know! That's all you care about, self! I'm sick! Sick to my bones! (*He pauses, takes out his wrist watch, reads the time and sighs. Very brief*

pause, and then, as if addressing some unseen force or voice, he gazes into space.) This house feels like fire! Who's doing all this! Mother, what is going on?

SHERIFAT:
I've already told you! Ask your wife!

DAISY: (*Flaring up again.*)
And I too have already told you to ask your mother. (*DAISY now goes into a rage.*) Nobody is asking Daisy anything! No way! I am not the cause of anything! And make no mistake about it! (*Car horn is heard outside.*)

OKEI: (*Calmly now.*)
Hmm . . . so, who is responsible?

DAISY:
Me? I can only speak for myself, and I know I'm not responsible. . . . (*The door swings open, and RUTH reenters. Another brief silence.*)

OKEI: (*Gasping.*)
Well, there goes the Queen of Feminism! There she goes! And with her cohort! And the circle is complete. Any need to ask questions? The answers are here in full regalia! Bravo, women! Salute to a world where women and trouble reign!! Anyone care to know the character of trouble? Where trouble comes from? (*OKEI begins to walk away.*)

RUTH: (*Haughtily.*)
Hmm . . . Daisy, is he okay? Does he need a drink or something? (*Silence. RUTH studies the tense atmosphere around her and makes her way toward a sofa.*) Who knows where trouble comes from? But I know it's certainly not from this end!

SHERIFAT:
And not from here either! Trouble travels with a hundred feet all at once. It never sleeps! Trouble works overtime to gain a stronghold. . . . (*Pause.*)

RUTH:
I don't know what you are talking about.

SHERIFAT: (*Coldly.*)
You do not know. And will never know!

RUTH:
As if you yourself know anything!

OKEI: (*Sternly to RUTH.*)
Now woman, you're overstepping your limit! THAT IS MY MOTHER! And I'm not going to sit here and fold my arms while

some half-baked, undeveloped . . . underdeveloped creature who calls herself woman insults my mother. . . .

SHERIFAT: *(Interrupting him.)*
No! Okei! Hold it! This is just child's play! I am not salt; I too can play in the rain! Who has ever heard that the metal gong was silenced? Who can silence the drums? No, Okei! Only a fowl runs from its own fart. Sherifat is too old and has been through too many storms to be blown by a mere wind. I can stand and take care of this myself. My feet are still too strong to need support. *(SHERIFAT stamps her feet one after the other on the floor.)* Can't you hear the thunder from my feet? I need no support! No, son. I have stood all these years on my feet. . . . I can still stand on my feet. Our ancestors are here! The earth is here! Yemoja is here! So how can I fall? No, son! Let the wind blow. It can only ruffle the feathers of the hen. Son, the wind blows, but it can only sway the reed from side to side. And that gives it strength to firm up its roots. It can't uproot the reed! So go, son, and leave me to take care of this myself! Leave yourself out of it. It's now between me and them!

RUTH:
So I see the battle is drawn. And I guess nobody's going to have a convulsion over this threat either. We'll see who laughs last. *(Silence.)*

OKEI: *(Resignedly sighing and walking toward the door leading out.)*
Well, I can see I'm an outsider here. And I have no place here anymore. Perhaps I should go back to my office. . . . *(OKEI picks up his briefcase and makes his way to the door, slamming it after him. Once OKEI departs, silence reigns.)*

RUTH: *(Coughing nervously and trying to break the silence.)*
Well, talk of trouble! Hmm . . . Mrs. Nweke, I hope you're not implying that I . . . I'm . . . the . . . the trouble? Do I bring trouble to your house?

SHERIFAT:
Thank God you now know that this too is my house! As for where trouble comes from, let the wise ones count their teeth with their tongue. Let them smell the odor of their mouth! *(Pause.)* And no one needs to tell them that their mouth stinks even to the extent that the vulture in the air would not touch their bodies for fear of poison!

RUTH:
Some creatures sure have a mouth! *(Silence. One can hear BOSE snoring in YEMOJA's arms. DAISY looks at her and instructs YEMOJA.)*

DAISY: (*Sighing.*)

Yemoja, put her to bed. I'm tired . . . tired . . . I'm tired! (*YEMOJA and SHERIFAT depart with BOSE while DAISY walks toward a sofa, clearly intending to throw herself onto it.*)

RUTH:

What a mess!

DAISY:

These women! Ruth, I feel trapped! When will this nightmare end? (*At this moment, YEMOJA and BOSE reenter, cross the living room and go outside. Neither DAISY nor RUTH says anything to them. YEMOJA is holding BOSE tenderly as they walk, with SHERIFAT following close behind them.*)

DAISY:

Yeah! . . . Ehm . . . a word with you. . . . (*Almost shouting.*) Ehm . . . yeah . . . a word with you!

SHERIFAT AND YEMOJA: (*Together.*)

A word with whom?

DAISY:

You!

SHERIFAT:

Hmm . . . Whoever "you" is should answer Her Highness!

DAISY:

Oh! I mean you . . . MAMA!

SHERIFAT: (*Laughing with scorn.*)

So I too have a name? I thought the mighty ones didn't know my name and had simply reduced me to a mere "you." So the poor too have a name?

DAISY:

Well, sorry if anyone gave you that impression. It wasn't intended. It's not our mission to . . . to . . .

SHERIFAT: (*Begins walking away.*)

Whatever your mission is, I'm on my way. We too have our own. . . .

DAISY:

Where are you going? (*Silence. SHERIFAT is at the door.*) Where are you going? . . . Walking into the night with my daughter? (*Silence.*) Where are you going . . . Ma . . . Ma. Mama, I need to talk with you. . . .

SHERIFAT:

When?

DAISY:

Now!

SHERIFAT:
>Hmm . . . why now? Not now! You can see we're set . . . and going somewhere . . . I cannot talk to you yet.

DAISY:
>When . . . when can we talk?

SHERIFAT:
>Later!

DAISY:
>Until then . . . we'll talk later then. . . . (SHERIFAT *slams the door after her. Silence.*)

RUTH:
>Well, my dear, I can see there have been changes here. And you have quite some characters! I tell you, your mother-in-law is something else! She needs to be sent to a reformatory, and your husband is emotionally underdeveloped. I know a lot of men like that. Okei is just typical . . . typical. But matched with your maid and mother-in-law? Ugh! Girl, you have a handful! More than a handful! Like being in a nursery. . . . I mean . . . I mean . . . I couldn't deal with all that garbage. Who needs all that aggravation? Nobody! And I know you don't have an inexhaustible store of patience to cope with these types of domestic animals. (*DAISY sighs.*) Well, don't worry, babe. It will soon be over.

DAISY:
>You think there's really any end in sight?

RUTH:
>Of course there is!

DAISY:
>How? When? Can't you see everything is getting out of control? We never bargained for this. And these village women are really shocking . . . you give them an inch, they want a mile.

RUTH:
>It won't be forever. Only temporary. For now, in order to get what we want, just use them. Use them! That's all! Stay calm . . . calm . . . cool . . . and indulge them for now until the program is launched. Then we'll know who the real boss is. I mean women. We'll know who the real women are, and who's in control. . . . (*The door opens.* SHERIFAT *returns, alone.*)

SHERIFAT:
>Now here I am! What do you want to talk about?

DAISY:
>Weee . . . we-men . . . about the women!

SHERIFAT:

Which women now? There are many. . . .

DAISY:

I mean those . . . the . . . the women from the village!

RUTH: *(Impatiently.)*

Daisy, go on. No mincing words. Tell her exactly who you're talking about!

DAISY:

The rural women! Women from Idu. . . .

SHERIFAT: *(Sarcastically.)*

Ohooh! Is that who you're talking about? Now I know! Ehm! Now I hear you! Tell me about them . . . these women of Idu. *(DAISY senses that her mother-in-law's mood is not right yet for discussion and chooses to remain silent. SHERIFAT continues.)* Hmm . . . why has everybody become silent all of a sudden? I thought I was summoned here to talk about the women? Or are you tired of telling? . . .

DAISY: *(As if waking from a reverie.)*

No! Ehm . . . seriously, Mama . . . ehm . . . forget about whatever has transpired between us. Let's put all that aside and mend fences . . . for the sake of women. You love them . . . I love them. . . . *(RUTH looks at DAISY.)* We . . . we love them! That is why you are here! That is why we are here . . . for them! We've done so much already. Don't let all the progress we have made go to waste! We'll be doing a disservice to the women.

RUTH:

And we can't afford to do that because we love them. . . .

SHERIFAT: *(Looking at RUTH suspiciously.)*

You love who? Which women?

RUTH:

The rural women!

SHERIFAT:

I see. That is the best thing my ears have heard in a very long time. . . . I see. . . . I hear. . . . The women will hear what you have to say to them. And we are not hard of hearing. Even these walls have ears! And walls do hear. . . . *(DAISY's confidence in being able to break the ice between her and her mother-in-law is now growing, and she begins to home in on this temporary victory.)*

DAISY:

I hear you . . . we hear you. That is why you are our mother! *(Looking first at RUTH, then turning to SHERIFAT.)* We are putting the women . . . everything . . . in your care.

RUTH: *(More flattering now.)*
    Oh, yes! You know best. And . . . eh . . . and . . . we . . . we . . . recognize your power over the women. . . .

SHERIFAT:
    For this visit. . . .

DAISY: *(Excitedly.)*
    Oh, yes! Oh, yes! We're rolling out the red carpet for them. . . .

RUTH:
    And the program will be launched as soon as this night is over. I will be leaving soon. Daisy, why don't you begin to teach them the marching steps while I go take care of some other business? Get Yemoja. Teach women how to march. You selected the cassette yet?

DAISY:
    Yes!

RUTH:
    Which one?

DAISY:
    A military tune; one that Her Excellency and the government can readily identify with.

RUTH:
    Wonderful! I trust your judgment! We'll be meeting later. . . . *(RUTH is already at the door.)*

DAISY:
    Okay, dear. We'll be together soon.

RUTH: *(Closing the door after her.)*
    Bye!

DAISY:
    Bye!

SHERIFAT:
    Bye bye, "Lutu"! *(DAISY takes a cassette tape from her bag. The Western military marching song begins to play, and DAISY joyfully hums along. She warms up to the tune and begins to add body movements. SHERIFAT observes, partly in amusement and partly out of curiosity.)*

DAISY: *(Marching.)*
    Yeah! This is it! This is it! The new step to learn. It's the step I must teach you. . . . Yeah! Try it! Try it, Mama! *(SHERIFAT clumsily tries to imitate the steps.)*

SHERIFAT: *(Marching awkwardly.)*
    Oh, these children! Leave my aging bones alone! How do you think my bones are going to bend to these?

DAISY: (*Still marching and panting.*)
> You'll see, Mama. It's so easy . . . so easy to change. It's easy to learn. . . .

SHERIFAT: (*Still imitating DAISY.*)
> And by the time we learn, our bones are broken. . . .

DAISY: (*Marching and panting.*)
> That too is necessary sometimes. But we learn. We learn. That's what matters in the end. The fractured bones will be put together and then we'll be whole again. (*The march increases in tempo.*) Yeah, Mama! You're doing it. We're doing it together. Where's Yemoja? (*Calling.*) Yemoja! Yemoja! Come out here! Come and learn the new steps! Yemojaaa!

YEMOJA: (*Running in and panting.*)
> Is everything okay?

DAISY: (*Still marching.*)
> Oh sure! Sure! Everything's okay, . . . (*She notices that SHERIFAT too is marching and is greatly amused by this.*)

YEMOJA:
> Ehn, our mother! You too?

SHERIFAT: (*Marching.*)
> Well, my child! What else do you expect me to do while I'm still here? The world is like a masquerade, changing, dancing, changing steps every time. If you want to see the dance fully, if you want to be an accountable witness, you must change your steps too. Isn't that what your new world calls for? I'm doing it! We're doing it! Yemoja, it's your turn. Join the dance. (*SHERIFAT pulls at YEMOJA's arm.*)

DAISY:
> Come on, Yemoja! Join! We're in this together. March! You got to prepare for tomorrow. The launching is tomorrow. (*YEMOJA timidly takes a step or two.*)

YEMOJA:
> It's so different!

DAISY:
> That is why you need time to learn it. Try! Go on trying. . . .

SHERIFAT:
> If, at my age, I can find myself doing this, you can too, Yemoja. You are young. And your bones are still soft. . . .

YEMOJA: (*Adjusting quickly to the tune.*)
> Maybe that is the problem with our younger generation. We are not strong enough. Our bones are too soft. . . . (*BOSE runs in calling.*)

BOSE:
> Mummy! Mummy! You have a telephone call!

DAISY:
> What?

BOSE:
> You have a call.

DAISY:
> From whom?

BOSE:
> It's . . . it's the . . . the minister.

DAISY:
> Okay, Bose. Run and tell him I'm in the middle of something. Tell him I'll call him back in a few minutes.

BOSE: *(Running out of the room.)*
> Okay, Mummy! *(Exit BOSE. DAISY soon stops and turns to SHERIFAT and YEMOJA.)*

DAISY:
> I must leave you now . . . I can see you're on your way. You don't need me to teach you anything, anymore. Just continue your rehearsal. . . . Practice! Practice! You need to rehearse. It's very important. You can't afford to disgrace yourselves tomorrow. You got to do women proud tomorrow! Just go on! I'm leaving. . . .

(DAISY is leaving while BOSE is coming back to join the women.)

BOSE:
> Mummy, can I join Grandma and Sissy in the march?

DAISY: *(Leaving.)*
> Sure! Why not?

BOSE:
> Because you get angry with me when I listen to Grandma's tales with Sissy Yemoja and when I join their drum dance. . . .

DAISY: *(Well on her way out now.)*
> This child! You are just impossible! I must leave now. Join them if you want to.

BOSE:
> Oh, thank you, Mummy! My Mummy is a good woman! Mummy's a good . . . *(She kisses her mother. DAISY is struggling to leave now so she can return the phone call from the minister. She disengages herself from BOSE and is hurrying to the door when BOSE shouts into the air.)* Muuuummmmy! *(DAISY turns, stops.)* Mummy, will I also join the women tomorrow at the launching?

DAISY:
> Hmm? What did you say?

BOSE:
> Mummy, I said, can I join the women tomorrow at the launching? (DAISY *studies her daughter briefly. She looks her straight in the eye, pulls her very close to her chin and speaks rather calmly.*)

DAISY:
> Bose, you are not in the women's league.

BOSE:
> I know. . . . I want . . .

DAISY: (*Screaming.*)
> BOOOSEEE!

BOSE:
> Yeeesss, Mummy!

DAISY: (*Calmly now.*)
> Bose, I know you're in Girl Guides. And you can march. . . . You can march here now, with the women . . . today . . . but not tomorrow. . . .

BOSE:
> Mummy . . .

DAISY: (*Impatiently.*)
> This child. STOP!! When will you find your place?

BOSE:
> I . . . will . . . Mummy, but . . . but . . . Mummy, you say it's not my turn yet. When will it be my turn?

DAISY:
> Oh, this child! Leave me alone! Can't you understand? You have to wait . . . WAIT! WHY CAN'T YOU WAIT? Child, you oppress me with your questions! Why are you so impatient?

BOSE:
> Mummy, I'm not impatient. It's just that you don't answer my questions, Mummy.

DAISY: (*Cuddling* BOSE.)
> I shall. . . . I will, child. . . .

BOSE:
> When?

DAISY:
> To . . . mo . . . rrow . . . tomorrow. . . .

BOSE:
> Tomorrow at what time?

TELL IT TO WOMEN

DAISY:
Tomorrow . . . just tomorrow!

BOSE:
Promise?

DAISY: *(Affirming.)*
Mmm . . .

BOSE:
Promise, Mummy?

DAISY: *(Disengaging herself from BOSE.)*
YEEESSS! Now Bose, off you go! Join the women!

BOSE:
But you say I'm not in the women's league. Why should I join them today and not tomorrow?

DAISY:
Tomorrow you'll find out. . . .

BOSE:
And that means tomorrow I will be in the women's league!

DAISY:
No!!

BOSE:
Why not? That's what you promised! Why not? Why? Why can't I be in the women's league? Why not . . . why not?

DAISY: *(Picking her words.)*
It's the women's . . . eh . . . it's . . . eh . . . women's turn . . . tomorrow. Not the turn of the Girl Guide. Bose, you must realize that you are just a child. . . .

BOSE: *(Protesting.)*
Mummy, I'm not a child! I'm ten years old!

DAISY:
Oh, yeah? We know Bose! An ancient woman in a ten-year-old body! We know that. But tomorrow is not your day. You will not join the women tomorrow. It's not a day for girls! It's a day for women! You'll have to wait for your turn. You can't jump the queue. There are many things you will learn and understand, tomorrow . . . but you must wait for your turn. . . . Okay, babe?

BOSE: *(Hesitating but nodding agreement.)*
Hmmmmm . . .

DAISY:
Go now and join the march . . . today. Only for today. I must leave you with them now. I must return the minister's call. Okay, babe?

BOSE:
> Yes, Mummy.

DAISY: *(Leaving.)*
> Go join the women.

BOSE: *(Running back to SHERIFAT and YEMOJA.)*
> Bye, Mummy!

DAISY:
> Goodbye, my babe! *(Exit DAISY. BOSE joins the women in rehearsal. At first she appears awkward in her movements, but soon her feet gain power.)*

YEMOJA:
> And we can do it better with the drum.

SHERIFAT: *(To BOSE.)*
> Go fetch the drum, my daughter! *(BOSE flies to get the drum and returns with it almost immediately. The dance now intensifies as SHERIFAT beats the drum for YEMOJA and BOSE.)*

YEMOJA:
> You see, our mother! We can change the steps!

SHERIFAT:
> We can! Thank God for daughters. . . .

YEMOJA:
> I'm excited!

BOSE:
> I am too. Grandma, Sissy Yemoja, is this tomorrow?

YEMOJA:
> Is tomorrow here?

BOSE:
> Yes, Sissy Yemoja.

YEMOJA:
> Hmm . . .

SHERIFAT: *(More attentively now.)*
> What? What does the child want to know?

YEMOJA:
> She wants to know if tomorrow is here.

SHERIFAT: *(Pause.)*
> Hmm . . . *(She looks at YEMOJA.)*

YEMOJA: *(To BOSE.)*
> Why do you ask?

BOSE:
> Because Mummy told me that tomorrow will soon be here.

TELL IT TO WOMEN

SHERIFAT:
: Of course, tomorrow will come.

BOSE:
: And that means I can dance with the women tomorrow? (*YEMOJA and SHERIFAT exchange glances. Silence.*)

SHERIFAT:
: Interesting . . . interesting. . . .

YEMOJA: (*As if waking up suddenly.*)
: Well, mother . . . why don't we let Bose dance with us tomorrow?

SHERIFAT:
: Why not? And we shall be doing the new yam festival ritual dance. . . .

YEMOJA: (*Lighting up.*)
: Which requires a maiden . . . a young daughter of Idu! (*BOSE's body is becoming more flexible. The women continue to learn the new movement.*)

YEMOJA:
: Boseee! So your mother lets you come to join us?

BOSE: (*Grinning.*)
: Yes.

YEMOJA:
: How nice. (*The women break up the rehearsal momentarily, and they sit in a circle on the floor.*)

SHERIFAT:
: Well, she can't do otherwise. Can't you see her mood is changing?

YEMOJA:
: Tell me about that. Why do you think she's changing . . . and being nice all of a sudden?

SHERIFAT:
: Well, I can't really put my finger on it. But I know things are no longer the same here. Maybe she's afraid. . . .

YEMOJA:
: Afraid of what? Who do those women fear?

SHERIFAT:
: Not even God! But who knows? Maybe she's afraid of losing face.

YEMOJA:
: Maybe. Especially now that the women are here.

SHERIFAT:
: Yes! And we're not alone anymore.

YEMOJA:
: Now let's get ready! The launching is tomorrow. We must be ready.

SHERIFAT:
>Oh, yes! We must be ready! Now let's continue the rehearsal. As she said, we must be prepared. (*She moves quickly, grabs* YEMOJA's *and* BOSE's *hands to resume the marching. They march briefly, with* YEMOJA *leading. Then, all of a sudden,* YEMOJA *stops, turns around and speaks.*)

YEMOJA:
>I have an idea!

SHERIFAT:
>What is it, my daughter?

YEMOJA:
>Why don't we do it this way?

SHERIFAT:
>How?

YEMOJA: (*Demonstrating.*)
>Let's do it like the ritual dance we do in Idu . . . you know the ritual dance for the new yam festival?

SHERIFAT:
>That's a great idea, my daughter! Yes, let's do it! (*They change the marching steps to the traditional dance steps. They are all visibly excited now. At first,* BOSE *is awkward in her movement, but soon her feet gain power.*)

SHERIFAT:
>Bose can do it. . . .

BOSE:
>I will! Let me dance, Grandmother!

SHERIFAT: (*To* YEMOJA.)
>You know we need two masquerades: one for the ritual dance to mark the new season . . . the new yam spirit, the other to mark the end of the old season. You can bear the mask of the old yam . . . the old season . . . only it's too heavy. I hope you can carry it . . .

BOSE: (*Interrupting.*)
>And I will be the other one . . . eh . . . the new yam?

SHERIFAT:
>My daughter, can you bear the mask of the new yam spirit?

BOSE:
>Yeess, Grandma! I can! I'm strong. (*She flexes her muscles.*)

SHERIFAT:
>Oh, that's my daughter! Daughter of Idu! Nwaomenka! Nwadiji! Nwa-mkpisi-aka-nete-lege-lege-mbosi ogu osie lim ike! Ede! Ajie! Ojogwu, my daughter! My husband! My mother! (SHERIFAT *is so empowered that she begins to drum exuberantly, and* YEMOJA *and* BOSE

dance in absolute frenzy until they grow tired and stop. SHERIFAT continues beating the drum slowly, gently, steadily.)

YEMOJA:
    It's great! The world will hear our footsteps tomorrow.

BOSE:
    And I will dance with the women tomorrow?

SHERIFAT:
    You will, my daughter. May the ancestors guide your feet!

YEMOJA:
    Iseeh!

BOSE:
    Iseeh!

YEMOJA:
    The women are here, our mother.

SHERIFAT:
    And we'll be leading the women tomorrow.

YEMOJA:
    Yes! We'd better hurry. Tomorrow is too near. . . .

SHERIFAT:
    It's here already!

YEMOJA:
    I have to run to meet the women.

SHERIFAT:
    It is important. We must brief them about this place . . . what is going on.

YEMOJA:
    And what to expect.

SHERIFAT:
    Well, hurry up then, my daughter. We cannot wait. Let Earth and Sea meet!

YEMOJA:
    Yes! Tomorrow, Earth and Sea will meet! (Exit YEMOJA.)

SHERIFAT:
    And you are the devotee of the goddess. . . .

BOSE:
    But there are two. Where's the devotee for the other one? Grandma, can you make me the devotee?

SHERIFAT:
    Who says you're not? You are already, my daughter.

BOSE: *(Excitedly.)*

Hurrah! I'm the devotee of . . . God! Grandma, I've become many things today: I'm the new . . . masquerade . . . I mean . . . eh . . . the new yam spirit. I'm the devotee of . . . of . . . the god . . . and so I'm many people. And I'm Bose too! Drum for me, Grandma! Mama, drum for me! *(She dances, dances, and her grandmother embraces her.)* But Grandma, I've heard you talk about the masquerade. I don't . . . fully understand. What's a masquerade, Grandma?

SHERIFAT: *(Carefully.)*

Hmm . . . a masquerade . . . masquerade. Now, how do I explain it? You are still very young. But . . . eh . . . hmm . . . let's put it this way. A masquerade is the symbol of the ancestors. . . . You know, the ancient ones: our great fathers and great mothers on earth . . . lying in earth? You remember what I told you before?

BOSE:

Hmm . . . some, not everything.

SHERIFAT:

You must remember this always: "Idu never dies."

BOSE:

What? I don't understand!

SHERIFAT:

I say that Idu people never die. We pass away, but we live forever. That is difficult for your young mind. But you will come to understand. Idu people never die! We may die in body; we do not die in spirit! When we get old, we return to earth to be born again. We remain there beneath the earth until we're born again as babies. That is why we pour libation on the earth. You've seen me do that often. When we eat or drink, we must always remember our mothers and fathers lying beneath the earth. Because they are not dead. They are still part of us. And they are the older members of our family.

BOSE:

I see. Now I know why you throw food and drink on the ground when you eat or pray. Now I know. But I wonder why my Mummy told me it was sinful . . . that you worship idols . . . and that you practice, practice . . . witch . . . witchcraft. *(She tries to restrain herself.)* Oh, Grandma, I hope you don't tell Mummy I said so. She'll kill me . . . be . . . cause she said I mustn't say it to anyone . . . not even to my Daddy. Because she said that you and Daddy are the same. *(Pause.)* Grandma, will you tell Mummy?

SHERIFAT:

Hmm . . . nooo! *(Pause.)*

BOSE:
Why do you think my Mummy talks like that?

SHERIFAT:
Child, what do you think your Mama knows? Like all these women of nowadays, your Mama reads and learns a lot of books . . . about other people, about many other things, but what does your Mama know about us? What does your Mama know about her own people? She's very ignorant, but she's too proud to realize it. It's sad . . . but that is what these women have become nowadays. And I'm glad you won't grow up to become one of them.

BOSE:
Grandma, are you angry with my Mummy?

SHERIFAT:
No!

BOSE:
But you two are always quarreling!

SHERIFAT:
I do not quarrel with your mother. The gods of Idu forbid that I do that. I only want her to see . . . see the difference. I want your mama to see us and her world from within . . . from inside us. Not from outside! Never from outside, for that is death!

BOSE:
But Grandma, you say we're Idu. And Idu people never die?

SHERIFAT:
Yes, we do not die except when we die young or if we get lost. . . . We do not die, especially if we depart this world when we are old.

BOSE:
But people die all the same, like . . . like the ants . . . I mean the ancestors . . . I mean our mothers and fathers on earth do not die?

SHERIFAT:
No, my child! They live forever.

BOSE: (*Excitedly.*)
I too would like to be an ancestor so I can live forever. I will be an ancestor!

SHERIFAT:
What else could you be, my daughter? You will live forever. The gods of Idu see that and hear that already! We must save some energy for tomorrow now. Let's go to bed and rest. (*They retire to the bedroom. Light dies down slowly and rises again.*)

MOVEMENT FIVE
Drums for Women

(*It's a new day. Everyone is fully awake as the sun rises, poking its fingers of flame across the face of the earth in this waking moment. The scene is an open space in the Sheraton hotel, where the rural women have been asked to assemble and line up for breakfast. Western classical music plays in the background. It is clear from their faces that they are bewildered by the affluent and extravagant decor. At first, everyone is so taken by the impressive surroundings that they remain mute until* ADAKU *breaks the silence.*)

ADAKU:
    I wonder where they are leading us to this time. And we are just following like sheep.

TOLUE:
    Well, our mother, let us be patient and just follow them. Don't you see everywhere is full of light here?

ADAKU:
    My daughters, I can see that. And maybe that is why I feel as if I'm walking in my sleep. My head is heavy. The journey has been too long. It has been like an endless journey.

TOLUE:
    And the road leading here is so long. Can you remember when we set out on this journey?

AJAKA:
    It's like trekking along a very long, narrow path on a very hot afternoon to reach the stream.

ADAKU:
    Think of the trekking and all that distance. And to think that you may finally get to the end of the road to find that the stream has been relocated. You cannot find tears. Your eyes are dry, stark dry like those of a rat that has fallen to the ground from the rooftop. That is perhaps the best way to describe what I feel inside me now. One moment, I feel something strange . . . like . . . like a huge lump lodged in my throat and waiting to burst any moment. Another moment, I feel like I am waking from a very long dream. . . . Everything

is so strange. There is too much light; I want to go back to sleep again.

TOLUE:
I too feel the same way, our mother. It's a nightmare . . . it's the way nightmares go.

ADAKU:
You said it right, my daughter! Nightmare! You wake up and there is too much light and you feel you're blind and this oppressive light mocks your blindness or wants to tear open the stitches in your eyes in a most uncharitable, rude way . . . just to make you realize the depth of your shortcomings.

AJAKA:
Hmm . . . that may be true. But I do not see it exactly the same way you are seeing it. Even a nightmare can show you what you can't see in the daytime.

ADAKU:
Nobody has said that it cannot. My concern is that I cannot tell where we are going or where they are leading us to now.

AJAKA:
They say they are leading us to eat. It is time to eat. That is where they are leading us. To eat! And if you ask again, they'll tell you exactly that, and that they didn't say it with water in their mouth either. And you know too that these Oyibo people do not open their mouths to talk . . . they grunt or speak, especially to us illiterate people, out of the corner of their mouth. What can you say? You cannot complain. After all, you cannot speak the white man's language. They can, and you can't tell them how the language must be spoken!

TOLUE:
Maybe they feel the words will disappear if they open their mouth too wide to say it. (*The women laugh.*)

AJAKA:
Yes, you must have closed lips to use the white man's tongue.

ADAKU:
I see! And is that why some child whose mother I still remember exactly the day she was born should come to us and ask us to follow without questioning? Without telling us where they are taking us to? And here we are, like a herd of cattle! My ancestors! They really amaze me! Hmm . . . (*ADAKU brings out ground tobacco from a container tucked under her wrapper and begins to poke it first into her nostrils and then into her mouth. Her lips and her entire visage now*

move with the vigor of a great suction mechanism, for ADAKU has paid some handsome dues to age with a number of her teeth.) But who am I to complain? Adaku is old and lacks the teeth to bite. So let those who can, devour the fufu and lick the soup as well! Who am I to complain? I have said it. Maybe I am now walking the crossroads between this world here and the world of our ancestors. I cannot wait. Everything is so strange here, and I just cannot wait for this journey to end.

TOLUE:

Our mother. We can understand how you feel . . . you in particular, who have walked so many other roads before now. It is hard, but what else is there to say but that the traveler must knot the bleeding umbilicus with patience? We can understand you are tired. It is not quite the same for us.

ADAKU:

Yes. Your bones are still strong and firm. You can hear the music of my bones like those of some rattle beads. I want to sleep. I am tired.

TOLUE:

Mother, you are just tired. It will soon be over, just stay with us. You need not say much or do much now. You have done too much for us already. This moment is very important to us, and your presence means so much. We need the wisdom of mothers like you to enable us to see through and beyond the tinted eyes of the city with their wild men and women who shade the malice and deceit in their eyes with glasses. With your wisdom of ages, you empower our eyes to look into the eyes of these tigers. And tell them, without trembling, exactly where we stand, and teach them that no one can push us around in spite of their learning.

ADAKU:

What learning? What do they know? Books! Let them go and sit down! Their books may only be good enough to wrap my pudding for the market!! (*She spits out her disgust while the other women laugh.*) Modern women? Tfia! Let me rest! What is modern about these so-called modern women? They are just as modern as some overnight shit from a loose bowel! DECADENT!! That is what they are! (*The other women are nearly hysterical with laughter.*) You see, my children, what I have come to understand about these modern people is that many of them are like large, half-filled barrels that leak from the bottom; the barrel soon dries out. That is why they must keep refilling their emptiness by going to school and returning to school to read this and that, because the so-called knowledge they acquire there is not their own. It's borrowed, like some undersize garment that you put on and it soon wears out or doesn't even fit your large frame. *(The women laugh.)*

TOLUE:
And that reminds me of a saying among our people: "You cannot sing and dance too loud in public when you are wearing a borrowed costume." *(The other women have already begun to laugh.)*

AJAKA:
Oh, yes! Because the owner of the costume may be too near for comfort.... *(The laughter continues.)*

ADAKU:
And may challenge you or even demand that you take off the costume right there and then. *(Heightened laughter among the women.)* That is the way I see the problem of people who show off with some borrowed tongue. They can never be masters.

AJAKA:
And even when they become adept, the owners are always nearby watching to see they do not perfect it beyond them.

TOLUE:
Or they easily change their codes to exclude you from the inside of things....

AJAKA:
And to ensure that you always remain a perpetual learner!

ADAKU:
That is the way I see these modern fairies with their book knowledge. Book knowledge is not life. Book people study life. We are the life! We are the story that they learn and tell about life! That is what I know, my children. And we cannot be ashamed to state what we know, for we are the spring and the fountain. These people are thirsting and searching for the root . . . for the source. So tell me what will become of our world if this spring . . . if the fountain dries up? What music will feed the soul of our world if the drums are silent? This is why we are here, my children. We have come a long way, and even if this is the last assignment I have to perform in my lifetime, I will do it . . . I must do it. That is the only reason I wait now. It may be painful, but it has been worth waiting for. As our people say, if you die while in search of the melon seed, it is a good thing that has killed you. Your death will not be for nothing. For the seed will grow, not for your benefit, but for the living and for posterity.

AJAKA:
That is very important.

ADAKU:
> I know. But my legs are failing me. I have been walking too long . . . and this place is getting too cold.

TOLUE:
> Oh, mother! It is the way of the modern! Their life is so hot they must freeze the air with machines so they do not burn too fast.

ADAKU:
> But they are already burning! And from both ends too! *(The women laugh again.)* You children can laugh as much as you choose, but that is the sad truth. And I don't see it any other way. How can any sensible person murder another when he or she will have to be the chief mourner? But that seems to be the way of the modern world. It is totally incomprehensible to me.

AJAKA: *(Laughing.)*
> They will have to explain it to you, mother.

ADAKU: *(Tersely.)*
> I will be gone by the time they are ready to explain. *(Pause.)* So, where do they say they are taking us to? Where are we going?

AJAKA:
> To eat.

ADAKU:
> I see. *(Pause.)* And we have to wait this long?

TOLUE:
> Well, let us be patient and watch them. Or maybe we can spend time discussing what we must tell them tomorrow. We cannot just swallow everything these people have to tell us, as if we are empty and totally ignorant about life.

AJAKA:
> You are right, my sister. These people need to be told what we know, where we are, and then they can meet us somewhere. We cannot just be running after them.

ADAKU:
> Never!

TOLUE:
> They have a lot to learn from us. . . .

AJAKA:
> That is true, and that is why we must not undervalue ourselves.

TOLUE:
> True!

ADAKU:
> And that is why we need a dialogue with these people! They cannot

just run into us and dump on us some half-digested garbage in the name of food. We must test this knowledge against the background of what we know already and see if it suits our stomach before we can swallow it. For all I know and feel, their food may be absolute poison, and in the end, we will be the worse for it.

AJAKA:

In that case, it is best that we remain with our hunger.

ADAKU:

As the saying goes, "if I cannot increase, let me remain as I am instead of diminishing!" We must always remember these wise sayings of old. And as with knives, sharpen our tongues with seven bars of salt for these people. Our own knives must be prepared to cut deep.

TOLUE:

It is good we have this opportunity to put our thoughts together. Today we should be able to speak as one unit. Not when Eke goes to Olu, Afor goes to Igbo! We must speak with one voice.

ADAKU:

And we are all ready. My children are wise!

TOLUE:

We must also remember that these people like to exaggerate and make simple things look too complex.

AJAKA:

Let them do as they like. As the saying goes, "there is no law binding the shoe-maker. Wherever he likes, he can strike his nails. . . ."

ADAKU:

Well, let them go on, so long as they don't stuff me with that trash they gave us yesterday on arrival. I know I am hungry, but I also know that I am not a goat to be fed with grass and raw trash. (*TOLUE and AJAKA laugh.*)

TOLUE:

It is not grass, mother. They call it "salada"!

ADAKU:

Let them be "sa-la-aa-da" there and learn to cook like proper women. I don't know when modern women will learn that cooking is an art that must be learnt and measured with grace and with care. These women should be told that cooking is not a matter of pour this, pour that! Salada . . . salanda . . . salamanda or whatever they call it. All is raw trash! I cannot be deceived. Let them invent all sorts of glorified names to mask the garbage. As we say, there is no amount of scrubbing that can brighten the dog's nose. It is black and will forever remain black. (*The women laugh.*)

TOLUE:

And what is more, they store these things in the cold for years until they are ready to be eaten.

ADAKU:

You see? So tell me why their men will not be impotent and the women sterile when all they eat has long been dead and buried in the cold!

TOLUE:

Is it only that? I hear that nowadays these women spend countless amounts of money to burn off fat. . . .

AJAKA:

Why won't they get bloated? Do they sweat? Struggle on the farm and go to the market as we do?

ADAKU:

They stay in their cold rooms and swell like pythons that have swallowed live goats.

TOLUE:

And there is always money to pay some wretched woman from the village to keep vigil . . . sleepless nights over their babies.

AJAKA:

Oh, Tolue! Don't remind me! The sight of pregnant educated women makes me sick! Oh, they are such a sight! *(She demonstrates, ridiculing the slouching motion of some overfed, pregnant, elitist woman. They laugh.)*

TOLUE:

And you remember that woman Dike's son brought home?

AJAKA:

Yes! The "moving house"? That was what she looked like!

TOLUE:

What was even more terrible, you know, we were almost going deaf while that woman was here. She screamed all day, calling their maid. Oh, poor Kam-for-tu! *(She demonstrates.)* Every day, Kam-for-tuuu! Kam-for-tuu. Bring my panty! Bring my bi-ra-zia! Oh, we were going deaf!

AJAKA:

And the funniest thing was that the panty and ba-ra-zia for which she wouldn't let Kamfortu rest were lying right at her feet! Right at her feet! She just couldn't get her mighty self down to pick them up.

TOLUE:

And she just lay there like some bread-loaf soaked in water! *(They laugh.)* Oh, my sisters! If I were a man, I would not accept food from these kinds of women!

ADAKU:

Indeed it is sad. These women today carry pregnancy as if it were some kind of disease. What? I cannot imagine that it is this same pregnancy we carried and ran and hoed and pounded yam and sold in the market with. These modern women turn everything into some kind of fetish!

AJAKA:

And the new fetish for them now is to slim down and look rope-like. Whoever told our women that thinness is a mark of beauty? Who wants "bonga" fish for a wife?

ADAKU:

Are they looking for bones? I have a huge store of them. *(The women laugh aloud.)* I can sell these my rattling bones for good money. And in exchange for the flesh they are paying so much to get rid of. I wish someone could tell women that they do not need to crush the life eggs that give them the power of womanhood.... I mean power. What else is greater power than that of womanhood? ... These new women must be told that the one power they have, and which no man can challenge or replicate, is that power of womanhood. Motherhood! The ultimate power of creation, that cannot be bought or bribed or sold or stolen by any man. It is no power any woman should give up out of foolishness, selfishness or shame!

TOLUE:

Motherhood is the ultimate power!

AJAKA:

And so is the kitchen!

TOLUE:

That too! That is where every woman must exercise absolute control. It is her sacred space, which no husband or male can violate!

AJAKA:

Yes! As far as the kitchen is concerned, husbands are strangers. Let my husband come into my kitchen and open my pot of soup and explain what he is doing there!

TOLUE:

The hand which exceeds the navel must explain its mission!

ADAKU:

My daughters, I am happy that you all see these things that churn my stomach about our modern women. How can being in the kitchen become an inferior act when it is for the kitchen and the stomach that a man labors?

AJAKA:
> And she is in absolute control! There is a saying that your bank is your stomach. And woman holds the key to that bank!

TOLUE:
> Ohooo! Tell that to our modern sisters!

ADAKU:
> And have they yet asked themselves why it is that only women sell in the marketplace? Women are in full control of the marketplace.

AJAKA:
> Yes, in Idu, women control the economy!

TOLUE:
> And our Omu is PRESIDENT of the marketplace.

AJAKA:
> Yes, no matter how powerful, the king cannot reign or exercise his control or powers in the marketplace. Only the Omu can. And our Omu is a woman among women! (*They surround ADAKU and look upon her with admiration.*)

TOLUE:
> Of course! She is the female king!

AJAKA:
> She holds the power to the economy!

TOLUE:
> What we must ask these women who think they know so much is to tell us what power is!

ADAKU:
> That is important! (*Pause.*) What is power? (*Silence.*)

TOLUE:
> Must one be a man to hold power?

AJAKA:
> What are the things a woman can do that a man cannot do?

ADAKU:
> Let the modern women tell us that!

TOLUE:
> And come to think of it, what do men work for?

AJAKA:
> For us and for our children!

TOLUE:
> Maybe that is why the nickname for married women is "Oliaku: The ones who enjoy the wealth of the world."

AJAKA:
> Yes, a man labors to please and serve one woman or another.

ADAKU:
> Well, that may not always be the case. But because a man feels inferior to a woman, or wants, or desires a woman, he may go all out and do the most unimaginable thing to please and win her over. But a man does that too only for a woman who is worth it. It is a true woman who knows who she is; proud of her womanhood. Not some creature who is straddling the fence and does not know whether she wants to be man or woman!

TOLUE:
> All I can say is that such women are sick.

AJAKA:
> They need a Do-kin-ta. *(The women laugh.)*

ADAKU:
> So tell me who holds the power in the household, if a man must harvest his yam and other produce and turn the best of it to his woman to take care of and control how and when it will be dispensed. I tell you, my children, I have not heard the sound of a school bell, not to mention going to school. But I tell you also that I do not need any school teacher to tell me where the real power lies in the family. A man who wants to die quickly should try to provoke his woman's wrath! Modern women do not know how much power they are losing by trying so hard to deny their natural rights of womanhood and the powers of motherhood. Let whoever wonders or doubts that power go and wake up our mothers from their graves and ask them what it was to be woman. What thunder it was to be woman! You women of nowadays need to find out what true power is! Must one be a king to hold power? To exercise power? What about king-makers? Ah, you women must go and think. And let me rest!

TOLUE:
> Our mother. This is the best truth we have heard in a very long time. These modern people are turning our world upside down.

ADAKU:
> And it will collapse on their heads!

TOLUE: *(Still laughing.)*
> Oh, our mother! It is so good to have you around us. You see so much and make us laugh. . . .

ADAKU:
> Yes, go on and laugh! Laugh while you still have your teeth and before they are taken away from you. Laugh while you still have the freedom, for the way I see things, a time will soon come when you

will have to pay for laughter. That is the world I see coming if nobody has the stomach to belch out this stinking truth now! There's still freedom to do so. When we get there, and they again offer us that sacrificial offering they call salada, then you will all know. I will bend down, pull my wrapper and then shit on it. Let anyone who wants to know the reason ask whoever gave me the garbage. Or better still, ask the one who gave it to me to eat it with my blessing. Nonsense! These people think they can just feed anyone with trash and walk away just like that as if they pass smoke from their buttocks! Let the rich feed on the ritual sacrifice they dispense to the poor and feel how nice and tasty it is to survive well in poverty!

TOLUE:

In spite of every . . .

AJAKA:

Yes, in spite of everything!

TOLUE:

Who will have dared give us sacrificial offerings?

ADAKU:

Well, you wait and see. I'm beginning to wonder where your pride has gone. You children of nowadays have done so much to shock my blinding eyes to wakefulness! Now tell me why elders like us should be here now tormenting our eyes with this naked light? And nobody, not even the ones who call themselves our daughters, who brought us here, has come to welcome us. Now and again someone comes and shouts at us from a distance, "Go there"! And we go. "Come here!" And we come.

TOLUE:

That is even better! The thing that pains me most is that I have a daughter in this city.

AJAKA:

That is true! Where is Yemoja?

ADAKU:

You are asking of Yemoja, who is still so young? What about Sherifat, a grandmother we sent here on our behalf to be our spokesperson? Has the city swallowed her up also?

AJAKA:

Well, I wouldn't be surprised. As you can see, the city has a hollow stomach, and it consumes all in its path.

ADAKU:

But that is not why a woman like Sherifat, an old woman, seasoned in our ways, should come here and forget herself. If that happens, what will be left of our world? What are we going to tell our children?

AJAKA:
That the city has a hot and hollow stomach? *(They laugh.)*

ADAKU:
Maybe that is why they have put that thing so close to us.

TOLUE:
What?

ADAKU:
That thing.

AJAKA:
Ohoooh! You mean that foto box?

ADAKU:
Yes.

AJAKA: *(Laughing.)*
That is fi . . . fi . . . dio . . . they call it fidio.

ADAKU:
I see! You say fidio?

AJAKA:
Yes! Fidio. That is one of the greatest wonders of the white man. I like it very much.

TOLUE:
That is the kind of thing we want them to bring to us to add to our lives instead of taking away what we have.

ADAKU:
Yes! They must bring what will have meaning to us! You people should help me tell them! These modern women—who walk and shake their buttocks, as if Adaku sits with her back and not her bottom! Tell them! Tell them too that Adaku has her bottom! It may not be fat or padded, but at least it is mine. Not borrowed. And I own it completely. And unlike these city women, I never walk and fear that my false bottom or false nails will fall off in public. *(The women are in an uproar of laughter now.)*

TOLUE:
Oh, our mother! You are so funny! We'll really miss you when you are gone! What you said just now reminds me of a story I once heard about this big expensive woman who kept the "Gofanor's Board" meeting waiting for hours one day because she woke up and couldn't find her eyelashes! *(The women become hysterical with laughter.)* I like them. One of the great wonders of the white man!

ADAKU:
> Wonders shall never cease among this new breed. We women of Idu are now too insignificant to be spoken to by our educated daughters. Or perhaps we have the white body of lepers. That is why our children must not be contaminated with white disease. That is why they must speak to us through foto boxes.

TOLUE:
> Well, I do not blame them. Sometimes I too feel that not being able to read and write is a disease.

ADAKU:
> As you say. But I too feel that they suffer from the reading and writing disease. Modern girls burn their men, bury them alive! And they think that is what gives them power!

TOLUE:
> Then they get married to pen and paper. . . .

AJAKA:
> Or marry some other woman, as I hear they do nowadays!

TOLUE:
> What about men marrying men?

ADAKU: (*Spitting in disgust.*)
> The GODS OF OUR LAND FORBID! Okpanam forbids ram!

AJAKA: (*Laughing.*)
> But they eat the ewe which gives birth to the ram!

ADAKU:
> Women sleeping with women . . . men sleeping with men? Tfia! Tfia! That is no subject of discussion in our world. Let it remain there in their world where it is now! What else is not found in their world? May my own eyes not see my own ears!

TOLUE AND AJAKA:
> Isseeeeh!!

ADAKU:
> Since they know so much, let their men give birth to babies!

TOLUE:
> That will be the day!

AJAKA:
> That will be the power!

ADAKU:
> That will be the death! (*Pause.*) Nonsense! Let us talk about the living, not about the dead! Boh! You people must not let me open my mouth or you will say Adaku has come again. But one thing I

must say for sure is that these people are turning the world upside down.

TOLUE:
You think our ancestors are asleep?

AJAKA:
NOOO! They see. They hear those who violate our Earth, our motherland.

ADAKU:
Why do you think they are being punished with incurable diseases?

TOLUE:
OHOOH! Since they know so much, let them explain it to us!

AJAKA:
Let them tell us why the rich too die, with all their power and money.

ADAKU:
My children! These modern people who claim to know so much and denounce our knowledge and our world have so much to explain. They have so much they must tell us. . . .

TOLUE:
And today is the beginning.

ADAKU:
Yes, today is the beginning. . . .

AJAKA:
Till then.

ADAKU:
But I'm tired. I cannot wait for this journey to end. I am tired. For now I am going to put tobacco in my mouth for my old bones to rest. Ajaka, let me have some tobacco if you still have any left. (*AJAKA gives her some ground tobacco, and she begins to lick it and spread it on her gums. Brief silence.*)

TOLUE:
So we are still here? Where are the women who brought us here?

AJAKA:
The women?

TOLUE:
When are they coming?

ADAKU: (*Mumbling through her tobacco-filled mouth.*)
They have forgotten us.

AJAKA:
Let us wait. . . .

ADAKU:
> What for?

AJAKA:
> For the modern women. . . .

ADAKU:
> I still don't know what for.

AJAKA:
> For them to tell us where we are going.

ADAKU: *(Laughing.)*
> Then you will go nowhere!

AJAKA:
> Why?

ADAKU:
> You'll see! They are just as blind as bats and pretending that they see far! I can see that even in my old age. Adaku sees farther than these modern women!

AJAKA:
> Do we start heading back home then?

TOLUE:
> How can we? When we have come this far? Our efforts must not be in vain.

AJAKA:
> So for how long must we wait?

ADAKU:
> For life . . . hmm . . . for eternity. . . .

TOLUE:
> Maybe not for that long. But I cannot hide that I am losing hope.

AJAKA:
> Let us have faith. They may remember us. . . .

ADAKU: *(Cynically.)*
> After we are gone. . . .

TOLUE: *(Vehemently.)*
> We'll make them remember us!

ADAKU:
> I feel abandoned!

TOLUE:
> I know, mother.

AJAKA:
> Let's be patient and not behave like women in the last months of

pregnancy. That is when the burden is greatest and the pangs make you grind your teeth.

TOLUE:
Yes! The last days of pregnancy are most horrifying!

ADAKU:
But you bear the pain because you know that, in the end, you'll give birth to a baby. And then you can see and feel the harvest of your pain.

AJAKA:
Yes. But this too is an experience. Let's not be like the tortoise who fell into a pit latrine for seven days, and, on the final day, when he was about to be rescued, he kept screaming, "Let me out of this mess! I can't stand the stench!"

TOLUE: *(Still laughing.)*
But he had been with that smell for "seven whole days"!

AJAKA:
Oh, life! That is the way of the world!!

ADAKU:
But we must face it.

TOLUE:
I have a feeling that Yemoja is coming. She knows we're here. She's my daughter and I know her. She can't stay there relaxed knowing that we are here. And no matter what happens, I am still her mother.

AJAKA:
And I am still her mother-in-law.

ADAKU:
Yemoja is a sensible girl. She won't do anything foolish.

TOLUE:
Why do you think we came to beg and reconcile with your family? We haven't seen Yemoja. She still has not come back home, but I know. And we know that she is a jewel among ornaments. Yemoja is the sweetest child any mother could hope to have. That is why I am here. That is why I do not feel eternal disgrace!

AJAKA:
And that is why our family was quick to forgive . . . or why do you think I'm here?

TOLUE:
I hear Koko and your husband, Ajie, are coming to witness the launching.

AJAKA:
Yes. The men have been left behind. But they too are on their way and will soon catch up with us. . . .

ADAKU:
>Especially since we haven't moved far since we left home.

TOLUE:
>Let them come and meet us. It will be a good gathering of the entire community.

ADAKU:
>That will be a rare kind of meeting. Because our worlds are so far apart and we never really get to meet in this way.

(General laughter from the women. Suddenly, an ultra-modern woman carrying files appears on the scene. The role of the LADY WITH FILES could be played by RUTH. Here she acts as the LADY WITH FILES, bearing pen and paper. She arrives at the scene, takes out a file and instructs the women to move from right to left. This leads to some confusion among the women.)

RUTH/LADY WITH FILES:
>Will you all move from there to here?

TOLUE AND AJAKA:
>What? *(The women look inquiringly at one another. It is obvious they are confused. ADAKU still sucks at her ground tobacco, relatively unconcerned with what is going on around her. In fact, she has spread one of her wrappers on the ground and is sitting on it.)*

RUTH/LADY WITH FILES:
>Will you all move from that place?

(The women move confusedly.)

AJAKA: *(Impatiently.)*
>Where are we moving to now? You are confusing us!

RUTH/LADY WITH FILES:
>Nobody is confusing you. It is just that you people don't understand anything and don't listen!

TOLUE: *(Angered.)*
>What?

RUTH/LADY WITH FILES:
>Eh . . . eh . . . all I'm asking you to do is to move from right to left. . . .

ADAKU: *(Sternly.)*
>Well, that is all you needed to say instead of insulting your head! We too, all of us here, have daughters and granddaughters like you. So how dare you? *(ADAKU turns to the women.)* My people, must we now, just because the "he-goat" also wears a beard, wake up in the morning and say to it "Good morning sir"?

Chorus of Women:
　　No!

Ruth/Lady with Files:
　　Well, I can see how you people feel. But I'm only doing my job. I'm simply following instructions. Soon the Rural Life Program will be launched. Our women leaders have asked you to change plans. They say I should tell you to wait for them.

Tolue:
　　What?

Ruth/Lady with Files:
　　The women are coming.

Chorus of Women:
　　Which women?

Ruth/Lady with Files:
　　THE WOMEN!

Chorus of Women:
　　Hmm . . .

Ruth/Lady with Files:
　　What do you mean, "hmm"?

Adaku:
　　"Hmm" means "hmm"! (*Tense silence.*)

Ruth/Lady with Files: (*Trying hard to control her anger toward these rude women.*)
　　Hmm . . . well, you have no choice but to obey simple instructions. Just do as you are told. No questions, and, of course, no more grunting "hmm." So now, move according to instruction. (*The women begin to move haphazardly—some this way, some that way—but Adaku defiantly sits where she is. The Lady with Files gives her an angry look but says nothing to her as she watches the other women attempting to adjust their position.*) Now stop and wait here! And note that you must conduct yourselves in an orderly fashion! Be quiet. . . . (*She is about to leave.*)

Tolue:
　　What?

Ruth/Lady with Files:
　　I say, be quiet. There are many important people in this hotel who are sleeping. Don't disturb them with your noise. (*Exit Ruth/Lady with Files.*)

Ajaka:
　　So we came all the way to the city to be silenced by these women?

TOLUE:
>That is the truth . . . too bitter to swallow. . . .

AJAKA: *(Hissing.)*
>These modern girls! *(She spits in disgust.)*

ADAKU: *(Calmly.)*
>But do you blame her? Can you blame anyone but yourselves? Will a rope which creeps across the footpath blame anyone but itself? That girl has no blame.

AJAKA:
>Why not?

TOLUE:
>Why not?

ADAKU:
>It is we who are to blame. *(Silence.)*

AJAKA:
>How?

ADAKU:
>We sold out . . . we sold ourselves . . . we sold our pride for the promise of this, their better life. . . . I mean momentary, material crumbs. We made ourselves look weak and cheap. *(Silence.)*

TOLUE:
>But that is no reason for them to take advantage of us. Imagine the insult!

ADAKU:
>I have said it! There is an underlying conspiracy against us. They are just using us. Didn't you hear her say she was acting on instruction? She was sent by the powers to insult us because we mean nothing to them. . . .

TOLUE: *(Interrupting.)*
>But as our people say, "The one who bears a rude message to the king is the one who insults the king."

ADAKU:
>Our people also say that the head does not fart but it is the head that bears the knock. Tell me, where are the people who sent for you? I am still waiting for someone to tell me where we are and where we are going. Are they not in this town? Do they not know we are here?

TOLUE:
>Maybe like the Oyibo people they are imitating, they are still sleeping in their beds . . .

ADAKU: *(Rising.)*
And making us old people wait for them to carry their fat buttocks out of the bed?

AJAKA:
Or maybe they think we are too insignificant to be seen.

ADAKU:
Withdraw that statement, Ajaka! Withdraw it!

AJAKA:
Well, our mother, bear with me. What else do you want me to say? How else are we to think or speak when our word means little or nothing to the people who matter nowadays?

ADAKU:
Well, you all think you're nothing. Then you are nothing! But I know that Adaku is somebody. I know who I am. If you have lost yourselves in this place because it is so vast and with too many lights that dazzle your vision, I, Adaku, know who I am and where I am coming from. I refuse to be blinded by too many lights. If you have, I will not! *(Brief silence.)*

TOLUE:
I know what our mother is saying and I believe in it. I tell you, since these women from the city came to Idu, everything has changed.

AJAKA:
Are you merely talking about change? Since they came to Idu, it is like a wild storm came to visit us.

TOLUE:
And the wind is blowing us out of place.

AJAKA:
Oh, my sister. We all feel the same way. But it is the way of the world nowadays. And all we can do is sit tight and live through it! We are living it! We are living it. Life is like watching a masquerade dance. If you want to see it clearly, you must move along with the masquerade. That is what our people say.

ADAKU:
And you must subject yourself to this kind of humiliation to watch the dance? If you are a part of the dance you would understand it better. If the drummers see us as active participants in the dance, they will not treat us as outsiders. But what I cannot understand is the fact that we allow ourselves to be used to create a new dance-step without respect or credit to us! I am tired. I wish we were never brought into this!

TOLUE:
I am beginning to wish that they never came to Idu. Our people pray

to the ancestors, "If we do not increase, at least let us remain as we are." But we are learning.

AJAKA:

Oh yes! We are learning new things!! That is the only good thing about this whole experience. We are learning the ways of these modern people.

TOLUE:

Their world is different.

AJAKA:

Hmm . . . their world is more than different. Modern women are strange. I do not know anymore what to call them. Women are no longer women.

TOLUE:

Are they men, then?

AJAKA:

Hmm . . . who knows? Maybe they want to be men. But I tell you, whatever they are, or want to be, their way of life no longer attracts me.

TOLUE:

I am happy that we have this opportunity to see things for ourselves.

AJAKA:

Scales are falling from our eyes. I can see now that we were blind. Blind as bats. . . .

ADAKU: *(As if waking from a reverie.)*

Blind? What do you mean by that?

TOLUE:

I mean we are blind . . . blind because we cannot read and write. . . .

ADAKU:

Well, maybe you are blind. I am not. You children allow yourselves to be blown by any wind. You baffle me. How can any daughter of Idu say we are blind? Because we cannot speak and write in other people's tongue? Do those people speak your own tongue? Why can we not hold what we have and be proud of it?

TOLUE:

No, our mother! You do not understand. What we are saying . . .

ADAKU: *(Angrily.)*

What is it you are saying?

AJAKA:

That these new people have power because they see far.

TOLUE:

And because they have acquired the magic of the white men.

ADAKU:
> We too have our own wisdom. We have our power. We have our own magic!

TOLUE:
> But look at the new power around us! They press one button, the ground moves. You do not walk, yet you are lifted up high, as if . . .

AJAKA:
> Oh, you mean that thing they call "alifeto"? Our mother, let us be honest. It is not that our place is not great, but there is a greater power. These white people have captured the world.

ADAKU:
> So why do they too die? If those new gods are that great, why have they not wiped out death? Doesn't it amaze you that the modern people are the ones who suffer the worst kinds of diseases? Remember what happened to Eke's son, who came back from Amilika with so much money? He died just like that: got swollen, and for that reason was buried in the bad bush. Such a shameful death! Like many of them die.

TOLUE:
> It is true what our mother said just now. It is amazing how the children of nowadays die just like that.

(The LADY WITH FILES *returns, pushing a trolley with various dishes of food before the women.*

RUTH/LADY WITH FILES:
> That is your meal. *(She exits.)*

AJAKA:
> Now that you say it, I am beginning to think I still cannot understand why we, in the village, with all our suffering, live longer than these people who have machines that feed them and they never have to lift their hands into their mouths.

TOLUE:
> And machines chew their meat for them too. *(They all laugh.)*

ADAKU:
> That is why they rot so easily. And their bones go too soft and rot so fast; they die too soon. Doesn't it amaze you how quickly our children of today turn grey?

TOLUE:
> Yes, our mother! Another good point! Why do they grey so fast nowadays?

AJAKA:
> And now you have so many aging mothers and fathers in the village burying their own children.

ADAKU: *(Opening her dish.)*

They have turned our world upside down. *(Pause.)* Now look at what they have put in front of you. *(The other women open their dishes.)* Now look at that and tell me what it is!

TOLUE:

It is Oyibo food. They grind the meat and serve it almost raw.

ADAKU: *(Looking nauseated.)*

And that is what they want Adaku to eat? Raw meat in her old age! I must now eat my meat with the blood to show that I am modern and civilized? *(She spits, disgusted.)* Ah! Adaku! You have lived too long! Small children must now hasten your death by feeding you with worms!

AJAKA:

I wonder why they must grind everything as if they are feeding newborn babies.

ADAKU:

That is not all. They put everything in the cold for years before they eat them. So tell me why they should not die slowly, if what they eat is so long dead? Tell me why our young men, whose blood should be hot and red, will not be impotent, and why the young women should not be sterile? I keep telling you children but nobody listens to me nowadays. As our people say, when the old woman speaks, it is as if her mouth is leaking like water being emptied into a basket. But I tell you, when it begins to take effect . . . Hmm!

AJAKA:

It is as dry as . . .

TOLUE:

Who says we are blind after all? Haven't you noticed that modern people have the worst kind of teeth? Look around you and you will see how many of them use false, artificial teeth.

AJAKA:

And they are green too! *(They all laugh.)*

TOLUE:

Hmm? The modern ones are very funny! You see a very rich, beautiful, expensive-looking person. In the day, the mouth is full of teeth. At night, it is empty. And the mouth moves with such sucking motion that an aged, toothless woman has a better grip than that of a child of . . .

AJAKA:

Who knows! The way these people chase after money nowadays? Some even sell their children and parents for money. And modern women?

ADAKU:
> Modern women? Hmm! What do they know about being woman?

TOLUE:
> They think being woman is brandishing a pen and using it to poke the eyes and faces of men and the poor . . .

ADAKU:
> If to be educated is to tear the family apart, stuff wool into the mouths of men, and dispense with children or kill them outright in the womb even before they can open their eyes to see the atrocities of modern women, I choose not to be educated.

TOLUE:
> And if they say that mothering is too burdensome and is an undesirable sign of illiteracy or underdevelopment, let them leave me with my own burden and not impose their vision of the world on me, as if I cannot see and choose for myself.

AJAKA:
> That is the point!

ADAKU:
> If they say they proclaim freedom, why will they not let me determine for myself what that freedom means?

TOLUE:
> Yes! Is there only one road to life?

AJAKA:
> Your purpose in life may not be mine even though we may be sisters. We can be friends, each one with her own Chi.

TOLUE:
> As our people way, "it may be the same mother that gives birth, but it may not be the same God that creates".

ADAKU:
> The destiny of the hen is not the destiny of the cock!

TOLUE:
> Let these people leave us alone!

ADAKU:
> Why must we all be forced to see the world with only their eyes? Are we blind?

AJAKA:
> Well, maybe it is not really a matter of blindness. . . .

ADAKU:
> But a matter of what?

AJAKA:
> Hmm . . .

TOLUE: *(Helping.)*
> But of difference....

ADAKU:
> NO! Leave her alone. Let her finish! I want to hear how she sees it. Go on, Ajaka! Tell us! Tell us how you see this issue!

AJAKA:
> What I am really concerned about is that these people think they have all the answers.

TOLUE:
> Yeeesss!

AJAKA:
> They think they know everything about the world . . . about life . . . that they must dictate to everybody how everything must be done.

TOLUE:
> What is right, and what is wrong....

ADAKU:
> Especially about our world....

AJAKA:
> And they forget that what may be good for them in their world may not be good for us in our world....

TOLUE:
> And what they see as suffering there may not be suffering here....

AJAKA:
> Precisely! Life is like that. Each one its own . . . each one its own season to bloom. It boils down to a question of seasons and times and times and tunes.

ADAKU:
> Absolutely! But most important, we must decide what our purpose is....

TOLUE:
> You mean our purpose in life?

ADAKU:
> Yes! That is what guides us. That is what guides our choices.

AJAKA:
> And the way we see the world. How to function in our world.

ADAKU:
> That is why we must not run after these new things just because they are new.

TOLUE:
> Then we must add one more request to these learned women....

ADAKU:
: What is life all about?

TOLUE:
: You took the question right from my mouth, our mother! Why are we here?

AJAKA:
: In the end, what do we want to accomplish?

TOLUE:
: I think . . . I think what we are really looking for is . . . is to add the wisdom of the new people to our own. You know, to get richer . . . in wisdom . . .

AJAKA:
: That for me is the better life!

TOLUE:
: That is THE BETTER LIFE! Not wiping out. But adding . . . adding new things to our life . . . not taking away the good things we already have for mere promises of value that is not yet tested. . . . *(Silence.)*

ADAKU:
: We have come a long way, my children. The journey has been long and painful but something has happened to me right here and now.

TOLUE:
: What is it, our mother?

ADAKU:
: Hmm . . . well, I feel different.

AJAKA AND TOLUE:
: How?

ADAKU:
: Hmm . . . it is not that easy to express. But . . . but . . . I feel like . . . we have accomplished something . . . something that feels new. I mean, I feel as if a weight has been lifted off my head and . . . and . . . we are going somewhere after all.

TOLUE:
: I feel that same way too.

AJAKA:
: Haven't I always told you that we will get there? That we will accomplish something on this mission?

ADAKU:
: At least it is good to know that all our search has not been in vain.

TOLUE:
: And that we have a clear vision of why we are here, what we believe in.

AJAKA:
: And let us not forget. This will also be an opportunity for us to see how other people see things in the world.

ADAKU:
: Yes! But we ask that they do not take away our sight. We want to be able to look at the world with many eyes.

TOLUE:
: So we are asking that they give us their eyes to add to our own eyes.

AJAKA:
: That we may see far and wide!

TOLUE: (*Laughing.*)
: Are we asking to be witches? Only witches see that far and wide from many sides. (*The women laugh.*)

ADAKU:
: If that is what it means to be a witch, I see nothing wrong with that. I can do with many more eyes . . . especially now that my own eyes are failing. We need more eyes to see the world fully. That is why we are here; to see the world better. And these women who say they have our interest at heart must realize this need, this special need. For us to know our own world, our life. What it is for us and what value it has for us. There is no other way.

AJAKA:
: No other way. Our world must be our center. We must tell that to the women. . . .

TOLUE:
: That is what to tell them. . . . That is what we must tell these women who walk on stilts. (*She begins to mock the ways and habits of elite women. She raises her buttocks like a jet about to take off and begins to strut on her toes.*)

TOLUE:
: They walk on stilts.

AJAKA:
: They talk "psi psi" like people chewing hot roasted yam in their mouths. (*General laughter among the women.*)

ADAKU:
: The new ways disgust me.

TOLUE:
: But they are attractive too. . . . (*Pointing at the hotel.*) Look at all the privileges!

ADAKU: (*Angrily.*)
: Yes, gold and silver! Scratch the surface, and see what lies beneath.

TOLUE:
> I admit they are shallow.

AJAKA:
> But . . .

ADAKU:
> But what?

AJAKA:
> Hmm . . . *(Pause.)* Still waters run deep. . . .

ADAKU:
> Not for us. Not for us whose feet know all the creeks. Not for us whose soles, for seasons, counted the grains of the sands of this Earth . . . our land, our Earth.

TOLUE: *(Excitedly.)*
> Not for us who are the Earth . . . and the Sea. . . . *(AJAKA excitedly joins them. They take up their drums and begin to dance. The women join hands, go round in circles, break up again and begin a mock courtship dance. AJAKA breaks away while ADAKU and TOLUE remain joined together in their dance.)*

AJAKA:
> Not when Earth and Sea meet and yield. . . . *(She returns to the "couple" and they all join hands and gyrate.)*

ADAKU:
> How can the Sea drown in shallow waters?

TOLUE:
> How can the Sea yield to a mere puddle?

AJAKA:
> How can the Earth yield to air? *(The women join and gyrate faster, when suddenly DAISY and RUTH storm onto the scene. At first the rural women are oblivious of their presence and continue the ritual dance. Daisy is incensed and tries to break away from the grip of RUTH, who attempts to moderate her temper. DAISY shouts at the women.)*

DAISY: *(Thunderously.)*
> NOW STOP! *(Sudden hush. Silence. The rural women still joined together freeze on one side, while DAISY and RUTH stand on the other, staring angrily at them like lionesses about to pounce on their prey. Breaking the silence.)* Now, what do you think you are doing? Where do you think you are? Look around. You think you are on your farms? Or the marketplace? Can't you see we have very important guests in this place?

RUTH: *(Intervening.)*
> Now hold it, love. It's not really as bad as you think. The VIPs may

find them interesting and exotic. You know? (*Daisy tries to say something again but Ruth is in the way. Ruth pulls Daisy aside and whispers something to her. Meanwhile, the rural women release one another but still stand together, dumbfounded by this drama of modernity. Ruth speaks persuasively.*) Our mothers. I'm surprised you're not tired after your long journey to the city. (*Silence.*) Eh . . . eh . . . well . . . how was the journey? (*Silence.*) Hmm . . . yes, I understand how you feel. You're tired because you've been traveling so long. (*Ruth goes over to the trolley where the food has been set for the women. She feels the side of one dish to test for warmth. To the women.*) Your food is getting cold. Why don't you come over here and eat while we take care of business? (*The women silently, mechanically, walk toward the trolley and sit down while Ruth returns to Daisy. The women begin to eat, but you can tell they hate the meal. Daisy and Ruth, aside now, confer.*) Hey, girl! Cheer up! It's not the end of the world!

DAISY:
It's so hard . . . so hard to break down these concrete walls. It's so hard to communicate when there are so many walls. Oh so many walls!

RUTH:
And that's why we must be strong. You can't hope to break walls with soft hands. You need faith to break walls. Never lose faith in yourself.

DAISY:
Not when you're dealing with the devil. And you see it working overtime to destroy you right in your face.

RUTH:
You gotta be strong! (*Brief silence.*) And remember this as a rule of thumb. When you eat with the devil, you gotta learn to eat with a very long spoon or the devil gonna get yea.

DAISY:
These rural creatures are devils!

RUTH:
Well, yes. But gods too must learn to give devils their due. Everything will soon be over. What you can't allow is to have this program flop.

DAISY:
That will be our death!

RUTH:
I'm glad you know that! You gotta be strong and stay strong to run against the currents. In a couple of hours, everything is gonna be

over. It's gonna be clear who is in control. So let's face the future. (DAISY *is calmer now.*)

DAISY:
Where do we go from here? And the men are here too . . .

RUTH:
Easy! Easy! Easy, Daisy! Everything's gonna be all right.

DAISY:
That's right.

RUTH: (*Hastily.*)
Get Yemoja and Sherifat. Their presence should change these women. There's too much change already. But they're their kind. We must admit we don't know these women as well as Yemoja and Sherifat. They understand one another. As Jimmy Cliff says, "You've gotta use what you've got to get what you need!" (*Still trying to console* DAISY, RUTH *sings a few lines of this tune and stops short.*) Understand, babe? Use what you've got.

DAISY: (*Pleased.*)
That's right. (*She looks at the clock.*) It's almost time. We've already taught Yemoja and Sherifat the marching song.

RUTH:
Go! Use the telephone. Go tell the women it's time. They should be here now. (DAISY *goes and picks up the telephone to invite* YEMOJA *and* SHERIFAT. *Meanwhile,* RUTH *continues singing Jimmy Cliff's "Use what you've got to get what you need." Soon* YEMOJA *and* SHERIFAT *arrive.* RUTH *and* DAISY *intercept them even before* YEMOJA *and* SHERIFAT *have a chance to interact with the other rural women.*)

DAISY: (*To* YEMOJA *and* SHERIFAT.)
Remember the purpose for which you were brought here: to move these women! The success of this launching depends on you. It's our project together. So tell it to the women.

RUTH:
Teach them the marching song. (*She looks at her watch.*) It's time for us to go. Everything is now in your hands. Daisy, let's go. (DAISY *and* RUTH *exit.* YEMOJA *and* SHERIFAT *cross over to the women.* AJAKA *is the first to notice their presence.*)

AJAKA:
Who are these ghosts? (*All eyes turn to* YEMOJA *and* SHERIFAT, *who smile awkwardly.* YEMOJA *and* SHERIFAT *go down on their knees as a mark of respect for* ADAKU, *their elder.* ADAKU *is adamant and silent, except when she sucks a bit at her tobacco. The ice is broken by the others.*)

TOLUE:
  Ehh! Now you remember we are here! (YEMOJA *genuflects to greet her mother.*)
AJAKA:
  So this is what the city does to people? Even the best of us?
TOLUE:
  You abandoned us. Eh?
YEMOJA: *(Pleading.)*
  Oh, no! Our mothers!
TOLUE: *(Ignoring her.)*
  And you? My age-grade Sherifat? You, whose umbilical cord was buried deep in the womb of the earth for so many years? Even you can come here and leave your roots to winds?
SHERIFAT: *(Pleading.)*
  No, Tolue! No! It's not that easy for plantain to grow as rapidly as yam. The season's wind is strong. My people, we need caution to walk in the wind. . . .
ADAKU: *(Breaking her silence.)*
  I can see that! So that is why you come here—to forget us?
YEMOJA AND SHERIFAT:
  No mother! How can we forget?
TOLUE:
  No! You did not forget. You were drowned in the sea. . . .
AJAKA:
  Silenced!
ADAKU:
  Hah! This new world! Each one fighting her own cause. That is why you too abandoned us to drown in this sea. Well, who should I blame but myself, who let myself be led by the nose? The rope which creeps into the footpath has no one to blame but itself. . . .
YEMOJA AND SHERIFAT:
  Forgive, our mother.
ADAKU:
  And you too, Yemoja? You too? The sea loses salt? Where then do we turn to?
YEMOJA:
  Forgive, mother. Forgive, our mothers! Times are hard and treacherous. But we must be strong. How are our people at home?
TOLUE:
  They are well. Your father, your husband, and everyone that matters in Idu are here already. They are in another hotel. I heard them say so a moment ago.

YEMOJA:
> Good! We'll all bear witness to this history. . . .

TOLUE:
> Tell us, what happened to you in the city?

YEMOJA:
> Not now. Not yet. Time shall come to tell it to women. As we say, it is not everything that a palm-wine tapper sees from the treetop that he tells.

SHERIFAT:
> The day is not as it was when the sun broke the face of the sky. So much heat, so many clouds. Oh, Adaku! It's so hard to travel when there's so much heat and rain threatening to combat the sky!

YEMOJA:
> How much faith is left the traveler unarmed without shield, without cover, when the rainbow spreads its jaws in the sky?

SHERIFAT:
> Mother, forgive us.

YEMOJA:
> Mothers, forgive us.

ADAKU: *(Calmly now.)*
> Hmm. You prick my mind. The sickness which prevents the rooster crowing at dawn must not be taken lightly.

TOLUE AND SHERIFAT:
> Must be serious indeed!

ADAKU: *(Blessing them.)*
> Arise, daughters! And join us!

YEMOJA AND SHERIFAT: *(Pointing at the food.)*
> It is so tasteless here. Now you have come, maybe your presence will bring the seasoning we need and long for. (*YEMOJA and SHERIFAT arise.*)

AJAKA:
> Now, tell us what you have learned.

ADAKU:
> We sent you here to be our eyes.

AJAKA:
> Tell us what you see.

TOLUE:
> Where next we are going.

ADAKU:
> Yemoja, speak!

YEMOJA:
> Our mother. How can I tell the story of a lifetime in one moment ... in one breath of air?

SHERIFAT:
> Mother, it has been a long road.

YEMOJA:
> A long journey to this place.

TOLUE AND AJAKA:
> Are you telling me? It's an endless road!

YEMOJA:
> Our mothers. There will be time to tell our story.

SHERIFAT:
> Oh, certainly! There will be time to tell and tell it over again for daughters yet unborn....

YEMOJA:
> There will be time....

ADAKU:
> For time is us. And we are the story....

SHERIFAT:
> That must be told.

ADAKU:
> Who else can tell our story but us?

AJAKA:
> Better than us?

YEMOJA:
> We are the story that must be told to history.

ADAKU: (*Excitedly.*)
> We now know what to tell the women today. We too have our own story.

AJAKA:
> Let no one tell it for us!

TOLUE:
> For we are the story!

ADAKU:
> Who can weave our story better than us?

AJAKA AND TOLUE:
> Who can weave our story better than us?

ADAKU:
> I du kwenu!

CHORUS OF WOMEN:
>Eei!

ADAKU:
>Kwenu!

CHORUS OF WOMEN:
>Eei! (*The women's excitement builds up, and* YEMOJA *falls at the feet of* ADAKU. *Brief silence.*)

SHERIFAT:
>Rise up, Yemoja, and lead us! As the women who led us here said, "Everything is now in your hands."

AJAKA:
>Lead us!

TOLUE:
>Teach us!

ADAKU:
>We are at the crossroads!

YEMOJA: (*Gleefully.*)
>Yes, our mothers. It is now clear to us that oil and water cannot blend.

AJAKA:
>These modern women!

TOLUE:
>Don't call them women! They are everything else but women!

AJAKA:
>See how they intimidate us? It's a season of silence.

ADAKU:
>NO!

YEMOJA: (*Excitedly.*)
>And I too say "No"! Our people have a saying, "If you say 'yes,' your Chi says 'yes.'"

TOLUE:
>Well said, our daughter. What else could be more powerful than one's own personal God?

ADAKU:
>EACH ONE WITH THEIR OWN GOD!

SHERIFAT:
>Whoever says that the pepper-fruit goes on a shameful journey?

TOLUE:
>Or that the drums are silent?

ADAKU:
: Well, the drum may seem silent.

YEMOJA:
: How come? How can the drums be silent when the gong is near to add voice to the drum?

ADAKU:
: Well said, our daughter! Now, my heart swells like the sea in high tide. Sherifat, Tolue, Ajaka, Yemoja, take up the drum to lead us. Lead the women! Drums for women! *(Slowly, the women begin some tunes with the drums, the gong and other instruments while YEMOJA speaks. At the same time, the women begin to pile up the artifacts and produce: yams, hand-woven cloths, garri, oil, nad so on, for which they have proverbial fame and prowess in their villages.)*

YEMOJA:
: We have the drum. We have our path . . . we know our path. They can take all else but not our drums.

CHORUS:
: And ask our feet to follow their road.

YEMOJA:
: We have our path, our feet are grounded in land and sea.

CHORUS:
: We drum! We dance! We drum and we dance!

YEMOJA:
: They cannot drown our steps with a marching song. Why must we abandon our own dance to match another's steps?

CHORUS:
: How can the squirrel's child be born dumb? We will not yield!

YEMOJA:
: We have our dance!

CHORUS:
: We have our drum!

YEMOJA:
: We are the Sea!

CHORUS:
: We are the Earth!

YEMOJA:
: How can wind drown Earth and Sea?

CHORUS:
: We are the land! *(Suddenly, BOSE runs in. She has been in search of YEMOJA and SHERIFAT.)*

BOSE:
> So here you are, Sissy YE-MO-JA! This is where you are? (YEMOJA *moves toward her and takes her by the hand.* BOSE *is panting.*) I have been searching for you.

YEMOJA:
> Really? Why?

BOSE:
> I thought you were gone.

YEMOJA:
> GONE?

BOSE: (*Nodding her head.*)
> Hmm!

YEMOJA:
> How can? How can I go when my mission is yet to be accomplished?

SHERIFAT:
> Child, how can we go when we are here to stay? (*Brief silence.*)

BOSE:
> I was . . . I was afraid. . . .

YEMOJA:
> Why?

SHERIFAT:
> Why?

BOSE: (*Hesitating.*)
> Hmm . . . because . . . because of my . . . Mummy. I know Mummy wants you to go. But I don't want you to go . . . Sissy Yemoja! Yemoja!

YEMOJA:
> Why? Why won't you let me go if your Mummy wants me to go?

BOSE:
> Because you are my good sister. And I know you. (*Silence.*) Promise me you will not go. Will you leave me, Sissy Yemoja? (*Brief silence.*)

YEMOJA: (*Affectionately.*)
> No, Bose! I will not leave you!

SHERIFAT: (*Cuddling* BOSE.)
> We are here together!

YEMOJA:
> No, my sweet one! I will not go! (*Pointing to the EARTH,* YEMOJA *makes a circle on the EARTH and turns to* BOSE.) Now see, my dear one? See! Take up this Earth. (BOSE *takes up a handful of sand.*) No, Bose! I do not mean the sand! I mean the Earth! I mean this circle!

I want you to lift the space . . . the circle! (BOSE *bends down again to try.*) Move it this way. . . .

BOSE:
How can I do it, Sissy? It's so hard! I can't. (*She bends down, tries harder, but lifts more sand.*) I can only take pieces of it. . . .

YEMOJA:
Ahh! My wise little one! THIS IS THE LAND! The land is here. Who can move the land?

SHERIFAT:
We are the land.

BOSE:
How?

SHERIFAT:
We are the Earth. . . . I mean we are part of the Earth and the Earth is part of us.

YEMOJA:
We are here to stay.

SHERIFAT:
And we hold our ground.

ADAKU:
You hear that child?

BOSE: (*Nodding.*)
Hmm . . .

YEMOJA:
What did Mama say?

BOSE:
We hold our ground! (*YEMOJA turns to the women.*)

YEMOJA:
You heard it! We are ready. It is time to drum! (*ADAKU takes up the drum. TOLUE follows.*) Now drum! Drum! (*Drum increases in tempo.*)

ADAKU:
Give power to our drums! (*Drum rises.*)

BOSE: (*Turning excitedly to YEMOJA.*)
Sissy, take my pen! Drum with my pen! (*YEMOJA takes up the pen and begins to drum. YEMOJA and the rest of the women become more and more empowered by the assertive rhythms of the drums. YEMOJA hands over her drum to AJAKA, who now drums along with the others while YEMOJA dances with Bose. The atmosphere is now charged with drumming and dancing. YEMOJA then unveils what she has brought with her and left on the ground while speaking with the women. One item is*

an effigy of the Earth Goddess, and the other is an effigy of Yemoja/ Onokwu, Goddess of the Sea, which she and SHERIFAT have prepared for this new day. They call these effigies the goddesses of the Old and the New Yam. YEMOJA lifts the Goddess of the New Yam and places it on BOSE's head. The other she puts on her own head.)

YEMOJA:
Bose! You bear up our spirit of the new yam! The season is here! *(The drums are calling. BOSE lifts it up and dances as if possessed. YEMOJA too dances frenziedly.)* This is what we must do when the moment comes. The launching is any moment now. Drums! Drums!

CHORUS:
DRUM FOR US! DRUMS! DRUMS!

YEMOJA:
FOR WOMEN!

CHORUS:
DRUMS FOR WOMEN! DRUMS! DRUMS! DRUMS! DRUMS FOR WOMEN!! *(They dance and dance, until a siren announces the arrival of Her Excellency. Then the drums are subdued by the sirens. The dance loses vigor as members of the VIP entourage arrive at the scene for the launching of the Better Life for Rural Women program. Sounds from the police sirens, clearing the road to secure the safety of Her Excellency, compete with the rhythm of the drums, until the latter is overpowered. Before the sirens completely overwhelm the drums, the rural women, together with BOSE, halt their dance and retire to their rooms in the hotel to get ready for this long-awaited event. Lights fade on them as they retire but soon come up again to reveal the colorful gathering of many important dignitaries: men, the elites, and women, who are seated on different rows or levels. On one side of the podium are the male representatives from the rural areas. DAISY's husband OKEI, KOKO, AJIE, YEMOJA's father OKEKE, and all the men we have encountered earlier are also present to bear witness to this final stage of the dance. The air sizzles with excitement. Full lights. The background music momentarily changes to a mixed sound of rock 'n' roll and Western classical music. OKEI goes over to AJIE and the other men from his village, to greet and welcome them.)*

AJIE: *(To OKEI.)*
So, you too have arrived, my son?

OKEI:
Yes, our father. I am here. What can men do?

AJIE:
Yes, my son. What can men do when women have taken over the stage?

OKEI:
: And they have the drums now!

AJIE:
: These women are strong.

OKEI:
: The women are here! (*OKEI turns to KOKO, who is talking with OKEKE, YEMOJA's father.*)

OKEKE:
: We are here at the service of our daughters?

KOKO:
: Yes, my in-law! We are here at the service of our women! This is their day! (*All the men herd together in a kind of semi-circle.*)

AJIE:
: Well, let's watch and see.

OKEKE:
: Yes! Let's see how the python will bask in the sunshine! (*The men laugh.*)

KOKO:
: We are mere witnesses.

OKEKE:
: Yes. And the stage is set . . . for women.

AJIE:
: Can you see them wielding the drum like a gun?

OKEKE:
: Hmm, my in-law! These women mean what they are saying!

AJIE:
: Let's see land and sea meet!

OKEI:
: Oh yes! We shall see!

AJIE:
: I'm glad to be alive to see this day.

KOKO:
: Who knows what to expect? Women are as unpredictable as the moon. Or why do you think the moon is associated with women's cycle?

AJIE:
: Who knows? As our people say, tomorrow is pregnant.

OKEKE:
: Indeed, tomorrow is pregnant. No one can predict what it will give birth to. . . .

AJIE:
> Male or female!

OKEI:
> What matters is that we gave them the chance. Let's see what they do with the freedom.

KOKO:
> Oh yes! We shall see! Is it these women whom I know?

OKEI:
> My brother. Are you telling me? It is women who will suffer. Women are harder on their fellow women.

KOKO:
> Very true.

AJIE:
> And as far as I can see, this whole movement will soon fade away in their eyes, just like any fine piece of cloth . . . just like any new fashion. I tell you, in my many years of life, I have not only come close to women, I KNOW WOMEN! Nothing lasts in their eyes.

KOKO:
> They'll drown in the sea of their freedom.

OKEI:
> But it is important that they experience this freedom. Women cannot now accuse us of standing in their way.

AJIE:
> Hmm . . . I have yet to find out what women are looking for. Can someone tell me, WHAT DO WOMEN WANT?

OKEKE:
> Ah, my in-law! You have taken the question right from my mouth. What do women want?

KOKO:
> Ah! Who knows?

OKEI:
> They will tell us today!

OKEKE:
> What do women want?

KOKO:
> To be men?

OKEKE:
> That will be the day!

AJIE:
> That question still plagues my mind. What do women want? We farm, our women get the best of the produce!

OKEKE:
> Women are like the Earth, they take . . . they drink and drink and never get filled. . . .

OKEI:
> But they too produce . . . give, just like the Earth.

OKEKE:
> That too is true.

AJIE:
> But it seems to me that now they want to take it all; all that they give.

OKEKE:
> And that will be sad. That is why they are mothers . . . I mean, like the Earth. And when they cannot give anymore, then what will become of our world?

AJIE:
> Ask me, my brother! Where will the world be without women? *(Silence.)*

KOKO:
> They know they are important. That is why they bluff so much. I mean, look at us now. What are we doing here but honoring our women? We have come all the way, from all corners of the earth to witness their . . . their . . .

OKEI:
> Homecoming!

KOKO:
> Yes! Their homecoming! *(Silence.)*

AJIE:
> All that they give. And women own the marketplace.

KOKO:
> I am absolutely convinced that our women underestimate their powers. Look, who is more powerful than the Omu of Idu? Can any man dare stand his ground in the marketplace?

OKEKE:
> You are asking that, does any man even have any space in the marketplace?

KOKO:
> Women control the marketplace of Idu. Where else could power lie?

AJIE:
> Let Ajaka tell me that there is no food for me in the house. Where will I go to?

Koko:
> It is clear our women do not know what they have.

Okei:
> And it is clear people don't know what they have until they lose it. Let them go on imitating all these wild women from the West.

Koko:
> I wonder if these women ever remember the role of the UMUADA of Idu when they talk about power. Who wields more power than the Umuada of Idu?

Ajie:
> Ask them! The women are here!

Okeke:
> And nowadays, women ride in long cars and splash water on us returning from the farm.

Koko:
> And are we not sweating and waiting here for a woman . . . Her Highness, the president's wife? What else do women want? To humiliate us before they know they have something? I tell you, I can no longer understand these women.

Ajie:
> I know what it is. They are taking too much liberty with our understanding.

Okeke:
> Now that president's wife, who keeps grown, able-bodied men like us waiting here for her, tell me, how many holes does she have between her thighs? Ten? *(The men laugh.)*

Koko:
> Who knows? She may have four breasts for all I care. These women are a special breed . . . not like our women of old.

Okei:
> A lot of them should not even bother being mothers because they lack the spirit of nurturing.

Koko:
> That too is true. I have been watching these people. They are too self-conscious, too self-centered, too much out for themselves. Our mothers gave us love unconditionally. These women make us pay for their love. . . .

Okei:
> And dearly too! *(Laughter increases among the men.)*

Ajie:
> Seriously, this is no laughing matter. Since this whole movement

started sweeping across our land, breaking down the roof tops, branches, uprooting the very soul of our land, my mind has been wrestling with this question. What do women want?

OKEI:
That is why we are here. Today women will tell us what they want!

AJIE:
Maybe I am getting too old. Since the many seasons of my life, I have never known any time to be this turbulent. These women are blowing us out of space like some hurricane.

OKEI:
It's no ordinary storm.

KOKO:
It's a whirlwind that does no one any good.

OKEI:
Well, we cannot dismiss it that way. The women may have some points. They have a case.

AJIE:
They do?

OKEI:
Oh, yes!

AJIE:
Well, you, my son, know the new ways. We do not. You know what the world today demands. And for that reason, let us believe that the women are right. But I must say one thing. Whatever it is they demand, these women are overdoing things. Our people have a saying, "One does not have to oversalt the soup to show that one is rich." Women are carrying this message about their emancipation too far. They have over-celebrated their cause. . . .

OKEKE:
Like children who score some good points in an argument against elders. They become intoxicated with their victory.

OKEI:
Well, this is their time. We must recognize it and that is why I am here. In fact, the president is here too in spirit. He has asked me to represent him. He is too busy with state matters. Let us wait and see what they do with the victory.

AJIE:
Oh, yes! It is not enough to win a war. One must learn to manage victory too.

OKEI:
Who will tell that to women?

TELL IT TO WOMEN

OKEKE:
What?

KOKO:
That it is not just enough to win. One must learn to manage victory. . . .

OKEKE:
Ohoo! Precisely! To win a war is not the victory. Management of victory is the victory.

CHORUS OF MEN:
Well, go tell it to women. (*Silence.*)

KOKO: (*To OKEI.*)
Are you not married to one of them? Go tell it to . . .

OKEI:
What about you? What are you doing here? Is Yemoja not your wife? Are you not here to celebrate with her?

OKEKE:
Celebrate what?

OKEI:
Their victory: the death of men and the birth of women. Isn't that clear enough?

AJIE:
Hmm . . .

OKEKE:
What do you mean "Hmm"?

AJIE:
Well, the question smells. I mean, is it not our collective tragedy?

KOKO:
In what way?

AJIE:
It is the death of the family. Women now turn into men, abandon the children to roam the streets. See my son's case now? Where is Yemoja gone? To the city! In search of what? I do not know!

KOKO:
Only women and their Chi know what they search for. Only they know what they want. I have no such power anymore to undress a woman and see what lies beneath. Women are just too deep nowadays, and we must learn to take them as we see them.

OKEI:
You mean unconditionally?

KOKO:
Yes! What else? If we want peace. Just surrender to them until they

get tired of bossing us around. You'll be surprised how much they'll miss us and look for us.

OKEI:

Why do you think even the ones who refuse to marry men marry their fellow women and yet reproduce the husband-wife relationship?

KOKO:

That too troubles my mind.

AJIE:

There is no evil one won't find among these modern people.

OKEKE:

The family boat is sinking, all because of women and their frivolities.

OKEI:

Hmm . . . my in-law. I do not quite agree with you on that note. There is something . . . I mean, a certain beauty in this women's movement. We cannot deny them that. . . . What I personally quarrel with is their excesses.

AJIE:

You can go on and call it anything. I am not convinced. Our women have always had freedom . . . freedom to do anything within the norms and values of our world. I do not see anything in this except these Oyibo people are inventing modern ways to ruin the family in a world they have already set adrift. That is all I can say. But you, my son, are one of them. You think like them. Why wouldn't you be on their side?

KOKO:

Who knows? His wife must have taken over his manhood. You can't trust these modern women.

AJIE:

In the end, we console ourselves, my son. Don't let's get carried away by this myth of women power. I am your father and I have seen storms worse than this one come and go. They may blow away many useful things, but storms do not last forever.

OKEKE:

Indeed, no season lasts forever.

AJIE:

This too shall pass away. . . . (*Suddenly the air is filled with military bugles.* OKEI *hurries back to his seat. The rural women, led by* YEMOJA, *have taken up their position facing the crowd. But* BOSE *is not with them now. Bugles continue until* HER EXCELLENCY *steps onto the podium, accompanied by* RUTH *and* DAISY. *All rise, until the powerful women take their positions. This is followed immediately by the playing of the national anthem.* DAISY, *as Director of Women's Affairs, moves to the microphone to address the gathering. Silence.)*

DAISY: *(Reading her speech.)*

This is the day! Women, this is your day! The day you have prepared for these many seasons! Let your voices rise! This is the day your voices must be heard! The period of silence is over! *(The women ululate.)* Today, we are privileged to have Her Excellency, respected wife of our president, take time off from her busy schedule to initiate us into this ritual: the launching of the Better Life for Rural Women program. Her Excellency is here in more than one capacity: as both the voice of the state and the voice of us whose knowledge, whose vision, has expanded tremendously with education from other lands. Our mothers have been blind, and that is why many things have passed them by. We have come to open their eyes to the new ways. We are the voice of our mothers. Let Her Excellency speak. *(Applause.* HER EXCELLENCY *rises. Her dress glitters in the sunlight. She speaks through an interpreter.)*

HER EXCELLENCY:

At last, the moment has come. This is the day that the Lord has made: FOR WOMEN! It is our time to be heard. For years, women's voices have been oppressed and marginalized, exploited and burdened in the patriarchal hierarchy of the feudalistic hegemony. Women are taking back what belongs to them: freedom, liberty and equality. Today we celebrate. We celebrate the liberty to excel without fear of oppression. We celebrate the right to equality. We celebrate the right to better living conditions. Today we celebrate women. It is a new beginning, when all women can come together in freedom, liberty and equality to be heard. We celebrate this Holy Trinity. Our mothers from the village are here. It is for them that we have this celebration. The victory today will be awarded to them for their sacrifice and understanding in raising daughters who go ahead of them and speak for them. For this reason, today is not our day, but the day of our mothers, who have gathered here to share with us the wealth of their experience. Above all, we thank them for their courage in giving us the voice to speak for them. A round of applause for our women! *(General applause.)* Now, my part is done. Let our mothers take the stage. *(Thunderous applause follows as* HER EXCELLENCY *sits.* YEMOJA *rises and stirs up the women. Drums fill the air for a few moments, then subside.* KOKO *is now very uneasy. He moves from his seat. He is obviously agitated.)*

YEMOJA: *(Composed, dignified, yet fiery.)*

Idu, Kwenu!

CHORUS OF VOICES:
> Eei!

YEMOJA:
> Kwenu!

CHORUS OF VOICES:
> Eei!

YEMOJA:
> Kwenu!

CHORUS OF VOICES:
> Eei!

YEMOJA: *(Pause.)*
> Today is the day long awaited. The women are here. The mothers are here! The drums are here! WHO CAN TAKE THE VOICE OF THE DRUM? *(This is followed by thunderous drumming from the rural women.)* The drums know what animal skin they come from. The drums know what beads and strings they are strung from. The drums move their tongues. Who can silence the drums? Who says the drums are silent? *(More thunderous drumming.)* The women are here! The mothers are here! They have the drums! They own the drums. Who else can speak for the drums?

CHORUS OF WOMEN:
> None that is born of woman! *(HER EXCELLENCY, DAISY, and RUTH are becoming fidgety now.)*

YEMOJA:
> Who has the power to slash the tongue of the drum and then talk in her place?

CHORUS OF WOMEN:
> None that is born of woman! *(Growing uneasiness among the elite women. DAISY and RUTH can be seen huddling together and conferring. YEMOJA continues her speech.)*

YEMOJA:
> Our drum is woman! Our drum is mother! Who says the drums are silent?

CHORUS OF WOMEN:
> The drums are here!

YEMOJA:
> The drums are here! We give way to the lead drum. Let her speak! We are the chorus of the drums! Let loose the tongue of the drum! *(YEMOJA returns to the crowd of women accompanied by thunderous applause and ululation from the rural women. ADAKU rises, her feeble frame firm and poised. She clears her throat, adjusts her wrapper, does*

a ritualistic cyclic, turn-around movement with her right hand raised in the air, and then begins a song, which the rural women respond to in chorus. It is a short song affirming the dignity of womanhood and motherhood. On the last note of the song, ADAKU, who has become strengthened and inspired almost to the point of possession, rouses the rural women.)

ADAKU:
Umuada, Daughters of Idu. Who makes this land?

CHORUS OF WOMEN:
We make the land!

ADAKU:
Who spoils the land?

CHORUS OF WOMEN:
We spoil the land!

ADAKU:
Kwenu!

CHORUS OF WOMEN:
Eei!

ADAKU:
Kwenu!

CHORUS OF WOMEN:
Eei!

ADAKU:
Kwenu!

CHORUS OF WOMEN:
Eei! *(Brief silence.)*

ADAKU: *(Continues.)*
Idu daughters and mothers! They say you are nothing. But you know you are the jewel of the land. You are the Earth. You are the Sea! How can man produce when Earth and Sea fight each other?

CHORUS OF WOMEN:
Never!

ADAKU:
How can a house divided against itself stand?

CHORUS OF WOMEN:
Never!

ADAKU:
Idu daughters and mothers, you are the treasure. They say you are suppressed but you know you are the salt of the land. Your umbilical cord is firmly planted in the roots of our land.

CHORUS OF WOMEN:
True, our mother!

ADAKU:
But they say you lack power. Who else knows you are the eternal womb of Earth but you? You are the wealth of the Sea. (*DAISY and RUTH show increasing uneasiness.*) But you know you have the yam. And you have the knife. How can anyone say you lack the power? Never! Through you, the Earth is reborn. Through you, the land is reborn. Through us the Sea gains its salt. Through woman, man comes to Earth. (*ADAKU begins to chant.*) Earth is woman. Woman is power. Power is Earth. Power is woman. Not measured in scales. Earth is power, not measured in scales.

CHORUS OF WOMEN: (*Intoning.*)
Earth is power! Power! Power! Earth is mother! Mother! Mother! Mother is power! Power! Power! Power is US! Power is woman!

ADAKU:
Idu daughters and mothers, they say your voice is silent. But you know you are the hen that crows to wake the rooster. You are the hen that crows to wake the rooster. How can day break without the voice of the rooster?

CHORUS OF WOMEN:
Woman is hen that crows to wake the rooster. Woman is hen that crows to wake the rooster.

ADAKU:
The rooster knows where his power comes from.

CHORUS OF WOMEN:
The rooster knows where his power lies.

ADAKU:
Are we not Umuada? Are we not daughters of Idu? Who else can hold the land in ransom but us? Are we not the seed yam from which the spirit of the land sprouts? Which man is born except from our womb?

CHORUS OF WOMEN:
Earth is power! Power! Power! Earth is mother! Mother! Mother! Mother is power! Power! Power! Power is us! Power is us! Power is us!

ADAKU:
Which man returns to Earth to join the ancestors without venerating the sacred daughters of the land? Who measures the power of woman in tin cans and metal spoons?

Chorus of Women:
Earth is power! Power! Power! Earth is mother! Mother! Mother! Mother is power! Power! Power! Power is us!

Adaku:
Only the uninitiated measure woman's power in cans and spoons!

Chorus of Women:
Only the uninitiated measure woman in scales. Only strangers do that. Only strangers do that. Only strangers lose sight of their bearings.

Adaku:
Ah! Strangers? Talk about strangers in the household! Talk about strangers in the family!

Chorus of Women:
Only strangers lose sight of their bearings. Only strangers lose sight of their bearings.

Adaku:
Yemoja! You know about strangers! You have been in the city. Tell us about strangers in the family. I am done. Yemoja, lead our drums! Idu, Kwenu!

Chorus of Women:
Eei! (*Drum accolades. Yemoja takes center stage. More drums and ululation from the women. As Yemoja speaks, mixed emotions play on the face of Koko, her husband. Sometimes his expression is one of agitation mingled with anger and anxiety. At other moments, it is one of exhilaration, pride, and admiration for his new "shero," this Yemoja he can still call his wife. Thus, as Yemoja begins to speak, Koko moves instinctively from one place to another and, in the process, trips on another man who almost has to hold him up to keep him from falling. Throughout this scene, Daisy and Ruth are thoroughly upset and disconcerted with the way these rural women have sabotaged their cause. Their anger intensifies when Yemoja takes her place majestically at the center of the half-moon shape formed by the women. The echoes provoked by Adaku's statement are still reverberating in the air when Yemoja, posed regally, casts her eye over the crowd, from one end to the other, and then rouses the women.*)

Yemoja:
Idu, Kwenu!

Chorus of Women:
Eei!

Yemoja:
Umuada, Kwenu!

CHORUS OF WOMEN:
> Eei!

YEMOJA:
> Kwenu!

CHORUS OF WOMEN:
> Eei!

YEMOJA:
> Kwenu!

CHORUS OF WOMEN:
> Eei!

YEMOJA:
> Umuada, who makes this land?

CHORUS OF WOMEN:
> We make the land!

YEMOJA:
> Who spoils the land?

CHORUS OF WOMEN:
> We spoil the land?.

YEMOJA: *(ululating.)*
> Eeeeeeeeei!

CHORUS OF WOMEN:
> Eeeeei! Eeeeei! Eeeeei! Eeeeei!

YEMOJA:
> Kwenu!

CHORUS OF WOMEN:
> Eeeeei!

YEMOJA:
> Kwenu!

CHORUS OF WOMEN:
> Eeeei!

YEMOJA:
> Kwezue nu!

CHORUS OF WOMEN:
> Eeei! *(Brief pause. YEMOJA, now transformed, speaks with the fire of conviction in her voice.)*

YEMOJA:
> Idu women! At last we all meet here after a long, tedious, tiring journey on the endlessly fast road to the city. We crossed many rivers to get here. We slapped and beat the face of the earth to get here. We trudged and trudged and trudged, our feet faltering, our fingers

missing, our toes missing to get to where we are now. Now, women, join hands, and together, with one voice, let us salute Ani, our own Goddess of the Earth, who held back her thirst that our blood might not wet her throat on this adventure to the city. *(The women perform a ritual of veneration to Earth.)* Let us salute Onokwu, our Yemoja, Goddess of the River and the Sea who kept the Earth supplied that our tears might not be squeezed out for water to purge this land, defiled, abused and violated by transgressors. *(The women perform the ritual of veneration to the Sea/River Goddess.)* Sherifat, our treasurer of memories! Spray the land with Nzu to revive the face and the beauty of this abused land. *(The women again, collectively, perform a ritual veneration to the Sea Goddess. Sherifat sprays Nzu, white clay, onto the Earth to placate her.)*

SHERIFAT: *(Invoking the goddesses.)*
Here! Take Nzu! You, Earth, our Goddess of the land, Eternal Mother, the mirror, whose face is never soiled! Your sons and daughters are here!

CHORUS:
Iseeeh!

SHERIFAT: *(Turning.)*
Yemoja! Go on! You are the mouth of the Earth! Tear off the strings that muffle the voice of the drum. Speak, Yemoja! The land awaits you! The land awaits your words! Your words are power.

CHORUS OF WOMEN:
Yemoja! Yemoja! Yemoja! Yemoja! Yemoja!

YEMOJA:
Idu women! There is a saying among our people that as the world moves with each new day, the hen gets a new husband. The sun is now overhead. The dews of the morning have cleared the clumsy sleep of waking, and the groping is gone. Our eyes are now so dry their heat glows enough to outshine the sun. The day is awake! We too are awake! Idu women, do I speak your voice?

CHORUS OF WOMEN:
You do!! Go on! Untie the sealed lips of the drums! *(Brief drum accolades follow, encouraging YEMOJA into action. Then silence.)*

YEMOJA:
Idu women! You who chart the sun's course from waking to when it sleeps in the evening! How can it be said your eyes are blind and you wander in the forest, when your hearts beat the rhythm of the season? Idu women! You, who are the womb of the Earth, from when the infant is planted, knowing where the infant's soul is

rooted. You, whose hands receive and return the human born from the earth. How can you accept that you lack power? How can you accept that you lack power?

CHORUS:
Never!

YEMOJA:
But they say you lack power!

CHORUS:
Who says we lack power?

YEMOJA:
They are here! The women are here!

CHORUS:
We know no such women! WE ARE THE WOMEN!

YEMOJA:
They say you lack power. What power is greater than the power of creation? Idu daughters, what name is stronger than the Umuada of Idu?

CHORUS:
None!!

YEMOJA:
But why then are you here? Are you not here because the ones who speak through their noses tell you that women are powerless? That you are used and abused?

CHORUS:
Never!

YEMOJA:
Who can silence the drum but the guinea fowl from the strange land? Yes, only the guinea fowl from the city can step on the face of the drum, my people!

CHORUS OF WOMEN:
Away with the guinea fowl! Away with the guinea fowl!

YEMOJA:
Idu women! You who know that all fowls that roam the forest, even the homegrown chicken, know their brood. The homegrown hen knows when to return home before dusk falls. The homegrown hen keeps her bearing when darkness is falling and takes her brood home. She spreads her wings over her brood. How then can she who knows her territory so well, knows where the hawk and kite hover in the sky to scavenge on her brood, lose her voice out of fear? Idu women! All fowls may look alike. But the homegrown hen is never mistaken for the guinea fowl that roams the forest, jumping from

one end of it to the other and never owning any place or space of her own. How can the guinea fowl take the place of the hen? Idu women! Do I speak your voice?

CHORUS OF WOMEN:
Go on, "drum"!

YEMOJA:
Drum for the women who are hard of hearing!! Drum! (*The women begin to sound their drums slowly but steadily.*) Idu women! It's now a whole season since the wild guinea fowl from the city flew into the nests and broke the eggs that were being nurtured for life. They tell you to throw away your men? Idu women! Do we, because the child messes up the bath throw him away with the bath water?

CHORUS:
No!

YEMOJA:
What happens to the plant with no root?

CHORUS OF WOMEN:
It withers, our sister!

YEMOJA:
It is now a whole season. The wild breed came to take us away from home to roam the jungle of the city. They told us our life was dull and controlled by men. Tell me, Idu women! Since we arrived here, what has become of us? Have we not been silenced . . . silenced not by others but by our own kind? Even more than ever before?

CHORUS OF WOMEN:
True, our sister!

YEMOJA:
Have we not gained new masters, deceptively speaking in feminine voices, and all in the name of liberation?

CHORUS OF WOMEN:
True, sister true!

YEMOJA:
Who now use and abuse us?

CHORUS OF WOMEN:
Our fellow women!

YEMOJA:
Who push us down and drown out our voices with the flow of their ink?

CHORUS OF WOMEN:
Our fellow women!

YEMOJA:
> Have we not exchanged our old masters for new ones, except they parade in the form of women?

CHORUS OF WOMEN:
> True, sister, true!

YEMOJA:
> Were we not lured to the slaughterhouse by our own kind?

CHORUS:
> Sister, that is the sad truth!

YEMOJA:
> So where then lies the difference? Where is the freedom modern women promise?

CHORUS OF WOMEN:
> We are still searching.

YEMOJA:
> I tell you, Idu women. It is early when the dark goat is chased back into its pen. So that it is not swallowed up by night. Mother Sherifat! You know it is a dangerous jungle here. We have seen and felt it together. We have a home. We have a place. Let us return to Idu, where we know the texture of the land, Mother Sherifat!

SHERIFAT: (*Excitedly.*)
> Yes, our daughter!

YEMOJA:
> You are the treasurer of the womb of earth. Go now. Lead us. Show the world our power to make and unmake the land. (*SHERIFAT unveils various produce from Idu that the women have brought: yams, cassava, beautiful hand-woven cloths and other things. The chorus of women begins to drum and ululate.*) Drums for women!! (*Drum quickens.*) Our royal mother, Adaku. You are Omu. You too hold court and council side by side with our male king. It is time. Show the world your staff of office. (*ADAKU stands, wielding her staff as Omu, female king who rules the marketplace and the economy of Idu.*) Women of Idu. What king rules over our Omu?

CHORUS OF WOMEN:
> None!

YEMOJA:
> What king is greater than our Omu?

CHORUS OF WOMEN:
> None!

YEMOJA:
> Aha! But the modern ones who claim we lack voices, the ones who

fly in from the strange lands and shout at us when they talk to us, they say they know us better than we do. Idu women! What does a guinea fowl know about being woman?

CHORUS OF WOMEN:
Nothing but images of women they see in the pond or pool!

YEMOJA:
What do they know about the line etchings of our lives? How much of our customs do they know?

CHORUS OF WOMEN:
What they hear from others!

YEMOJA:
Tell me, daughters of Idu. These ones who now take over your voices and speak for you women, are they close to Earth? Can they tell when the womb of the Earth turns? When she labors? When she bleeds? When the souls of plants change in tune with the Earth? But you Idu women know and feel the texture of the Earth. You breathe the air of the seasons. How then can you allow your voices to be muffled in the wind?

CHORUS OF WOMEN:
Never!

YEMOJA:
Who are these so-called women who switch off the cries of infants and replace them with radio cassettes? Tell me, Idu women, whether to age is to die.

CHORUS OF WOMEN: (*Chanting.*)
To age is not to die! It is the season's cycle! It is the world's rhythm! To age is not to die! To die is not to die! It is nature's power of rebirth! Not power measured in scales! Not power measured in scales! It is the power of life! It is the power of life!

YEMOJA:
So where is power in the jungle city where you have no place? Where you have no hold? Women, welcome to the jungle, where you lose your tongue and others speak for you!

CHORUS OF WOMEN: (*More agitated now.*)
NO! Away with jungles! Away with the jungle! We have our home! We know our place! Away with silence! We have our drums.

YEMOJA:
Let no one speak FOR US! Mother Sherifat, treasurer of the womb of earth, unmask the face of our soul. Let the drums speak! (*As SHERIFAT unmasks the effigies, the drums take over the space. The women are now highly charged and empowered, and they dance. By*

this time, RUTH and DAISY are fuming and burning silently. DAISY is so angry that as she absentmindedly fiddles with the champagne glass placed in front of her to toast their new achievement, the glass suddenly slips from her fingers and shatters into pieces on the table. She freezes, as an aide-de-camp attempts to clear the mess on the table. Everything is now still. YEMOJA holds her breath for a brief moment, waiting for the rumblings to die down, then with all her power and majesty speaks.) Get ready to hold up your image and sharpen your tongue for the world. Idu women, who will lead the new dance? We have the tongue. We have the drum. We own the word. We own the drum. Let the drum speak! *(Silence. Tension fills the air. The drums gradually begin to throb. As Yemoja makes her pronouncement, BOSE jumps like a lightning flash onto center stage. She dances. She dances with grace and ferocity, yet with a well-coordinated motion. ADAKU takes up the effigy of the new yam spirit and begins to place it on BOSE's head. YEMOJA lifts the other effigy onto her own head and joins BOSE in the feverish dance. Other women join too. The dance intensifies. Everything happens with lightning speed as music and dance rise to a crescendo. ADAKU then lifts the mask in front of everyone, revealing BOSE. Suddenly screams compete with the drums.)*

DAISY:
Nooooooo! NOT MY OWN DAAAUUGHHHTER!!

RUTH: *(Shouts.)*
Sabotage! *(RUTH is now up and so is DAISY, who is still screaming for her daughter. But the drums have gained such power and such eloquence that their protest is drowned out. The dance rises to fever pitch. As DAISY dashes toward BOSE, the women encircle them. RUTH is quaking with anger and trying to run from the arena, but the women lay hold of her. BOSE now dances toward her father, OKEI, and the other elders as a mark of traditional salute and respect. Her father responds by blessing her and joining in the dance. KOKO, YEMOJA's husband, has become so overwhelmed by his wife's new strength that he is drawn to her as she dances gracefully in the public arena. This new mood causes a stir in the crowd. Meanwhile, in the confusion, RUTH breaks free of the women's grasp and tries to escape, but ADAKU spots her in time and tries to grab her. RUTH falls on ADAKU, crushing the old woman to death and injuring herself. RUTH lies choking on the ground, but in the frenzy, no one notices. As KOKO meets YEMOJA, BOSE and OKEI meet DAISY, who is now completely shaken. YEMOJA moves forward with a sweeping motion, with KOKO dancing behind her. She lifts the effigy from BOSE's head and places it on DAISY's head. The women then ululate, drum and chant, "Yemoja! Yemoja! Yemoja! Yemoja." The atmosphere is wild with women, drumming and chanting: "Yemoja! Yemoja!".)*

YEMOJA:
> Dance, Daisy! Daisy, dance! *(The women take up the chorus.)*

CHORUS OF WOMEN:
> Dance, Daazi! Daazi, dance! Dance, Daazi! Daazi, dance! Yemoja! Yemoja! Yemoja!

YEMOJA:
> Drums for women!

CHORUS OF WOMEN:
> Yemoja! Yemoja! Yemoja! *(The music swells. KOKO embraces YEMOJA at one side of the stage. OKEI, BOSE, and DAISY form a cluster at center stage. YEMOJA's mother, father and her entire extended family together with that of OKEI join in the dance. Echoes of "Yemoja! Yemoja!" still fill the air when suddenly BOSE spots ADAKU's lifeless body on the ground and RUTH hovering over her. A hush falls over the crowd. BOSE, alarmed, screams.)*

BOSE:
> Maaaammmmmmmaaaa Adakuuuuuu

DAISY:
> RUUUUUUTHHHHH. *(Everyone turns in the direction she's pointing. The drums are silent following the child's anguished cry. People rush to the scene immediately but ADAKU is already dead and RUTH is suffocating. The siren sounds of an ambulance can be heard. The ambulance arrives, and RUTH is whisked into it. All the Idu men and women form a circle around the body of ADAKU as they prepare to lift her up. The slow, mournful notes of a flute are heard. Once ADAKU's body is aloft, a drum accompanies the flute slowly but steadily until the music intensifies and the Idu people dance to the frenetic rhythm until sudden BLACKOUT.)*

www.ingramcontent.com/pod-product-compliance
Lightning Source LLC
Chambersburg PA
CBHW050526170426
43201CB00013B/2095